Vickers
1911–77

Books

AVIATION INDUSTRY SERIES, VOLUME 4

Back cover image: A Wellesley Mk I.

Title page image: The first 800 series Viscount built was G-AOJA, pictured, being put through its paces before delivery to BEA in 1956. The aircraft was lost on 23 October 1957, when it crashed at Nutts Corner in poor weather conditions with the loss of all seven on board. (*Aeroplane*)

Contents page image: The beautiful Vickers VC10, pictured during its heyday with BOAC. (*Aeroplane*)

Published by Key Books
An imprint of Key Publishing Ltd
PO Box 100
Stamford
Lincs PE9 1XQ

www.keypublishing.com

Original edition published as *Vickers Company Profile 1911–77* © 2012, edited by Martyn Chorlton

This edition © 2022

ISBN 978 1 80282 369 1

Typeset by SJmagic DESIGN SERVICES, India.

Contents

The Vickers Story

The novel world of military aviation first caught the attention of Vickers, Sons and Maxim at the beginning of the 20th century, when powered dirigible-type balloons began to grace the sky, and the Wright Brothers achieved the first flight in a heavier-than-air machine, in a controlled manner, in 1903.

The first aviation project that Vickers embarked on was in 1908, when the Admiralty requested a big rigid airship in response to the great progress the Germans were making with their Zeppelins. The giant airship, ironically named the 'Mayfly', was destined to be a failure, but this did not put the company off the subject, and in 1911, the same year that the airship broke in two at Barrow, Vickers established an aviation department at Brooklands. Its role was to design and build aircraft, and, not long after, a flying school was also established.

Vickers' aviation interests steadily expanded beyond its already established locations, opening a facility in Erith in Kent, which began aircraft construction, and a specialised drawing office at Vickers House, Broadway, Westminster. On the recommendation of Capt Herbert F. Wood, Vickers managed to negotiate a licence with Robert Esnault Pelterie of Billancourt, Seine, to sell aircraft and engines of the R.E.P. type and design. Capt Murray Sueter, RN, the Admiralty Inspecting Captain of Airships, endorsed the R.E.Ps, describing them as 'outstanding examples of French design'. Sueter also suggested to Vickers that the Admiralty might be interested in buying R.E.Ps as naval military machines.

This was certainly advanced thinking, because in 1911 the Admiralty had no intention of buying aircraft, but this did not stop Vickers from purchasing a single French-built R.E.P. for demonstration purposes and the rear fuselage of another. The latter was incorporated into the first Vickers aircraft, named simply No. 1 monoplane. The aircraft was redesigned by draughtsman Archibald R. Low and engineer George H. Challenger. The pilot was Leslie F. Macdonald from the British and Colonial Aeroplane Company; later, aircraft designer and manufacturer in his own right, Howard Flanders also joined the team at Brooklands.

The basic design of the R.E.P. was more pioneering than it may appear at first glance; its steel-tube construction and, just as significantly, its single control-column method of flying the aircraft, has remained the same ever since. Its inventor, Pelterie, subsequently claimed successfully against Vickers for the sum of £40,000 for using his control system, but he was never that successful against the host of aircraft manufacturers that followed suit.

The second aircraft to be built by Vickers was the No. 2 monoplane, which was sold to the 1912 Australian Antarctic expedition, while others were gainfully employed by the new Vickers Flying School at Brooklands. The latter was no exception in introducing the new generation of pusher

Affectionately nicknamed the 'Wimpy', after J. Wellington Wimpy of Popeye fame, the Wellington was a remarkable success for both Vickers and the country. The bomber provided the backbone of Bomber Command during the early stages of World War Two. This is Wellington Mk III, X3763, of 425 Squadron. (*Aeroplane*)

Above: A good example of the cross-section of different aircraft types at Joyce Green. From left to right, an F.B.12, F.B.14, F.B.11 and F.B.16.

Right: By establishing itself within the confines of the famous banked motor racing circuit at Brooklands, which opened in 1907, the fledgling Vickers quickly found itself at the centre of the beating heart of British aviation.

biplanes, all of which were generally descended from the Farman design. Vickers produced its own modified version, which was virtually the same as the Bristol Boxkite. Locating the engine at the back of the aircraft was quickly seen by the Vickers' designers as ideal for having a forward-firing machine gun fitted, with an uninterrupted field of fire. This period prompted hundreds of designs to be produced by Vickers, including many for the German government, which were quickly withdrawn in August 1914.

On the outbreak of World War One, Vickers, like all other aircraft manufacturers of the day, were allocated contracts from the War Office or the Admiralty, the latter having quickly come around to the idea that having aircraft was a necessity. Orders for the B.E.2 and the B.E.2A were received, all of them being built at Erith.

Prolific design output

August 1914 also saw the arrival of Rex K. Pierson, a former engineering apprentice, who was appointed as chief designer, a role he would continue for another 28 years. The Vickers' design office was also relocated to the Crayford works, along with the bulk of aircraft manufacturing.

Vickers then began producing a host of designs in response to the main requirements of the Royal Naval Air Service (RNAS) and the Royal Flying Corps (RFC), although the majority of these aircraft were not successful, and orders were few and far between. Flight test reports of the machines that did make it to the Central Flying School (CFS) at Upavon and the Aeroplane & Armament Experimental Establishment (A&AEE) at Martlesham Heath were rarely favourable.

One of the great successes for Vickers during World War One began in July 1917, when the Air Board made a request for a new long-range bomber powered by a pair of Hispano-Suiza engines. Conveniently, Pierson had already designed the smaller twin-engined F.B.8, which itself was a development of the Flanders-designed F.B.7. Intended as a fighter, the F.B.8 was a failure simply because its performance and general capability was no better than its single-engined contemporaries; however, its design would provide the core for the new F.B.27, later to be known as the Vimy. First flown with Hispano-Suiza engines, by Capt Gordon Bell on 20 November 1917, the reliable Rolls-Royce Eagle was later fitted into the production variant, the F.B.27A. The Vimy would prove to be one of those iconic aircraft in the history of aviation, its place secured when Alcock and Brown first flew non-stop across the Atlantic in June 1919.

A decline in military orders

Following the Armistice, military aircraft contracts were cut to the core, resulting in many young aircraft manufacturers falling by the wayside. Vickers decided to regroup its aircraft manufacturing by moving its main operation from Crayford and the design department from Imperial Court, Knightsbridge (located there since 1916), to Weybridge, where it would remain until the end. The latter was placed in Pinewood House, which was where the works manager, Percy Maxwell-Muller, had lived during the war. The house, which was located within the Weybridge plant, was bought by Vickers after the war.

By late 1918, the Weybridge factory was firmly under the control of the aviation department of Vickers Ltd, which was now under the management of Capt Peter Dyke Acland. He had succeeded Maj Wood, who had fallen victim to the flu pandemic that claimed almost 5 per cent of the world's population in 1918. Full credit should be given to Maj Wood, who established Vickers' aviation thanks to his efforts with French aircraft manufacturers.

Aircraft production remained in the doldrums during the early 1920s, but took a turn for the better in 1924. By this time, production of the Vimy, Vernon and Viking started to gather momentum, and once healthy orders for the Virginia heavy bomber and the Victoria bomber-transport had been received, Vickers' inter-war workload was secure.

During the post-World War One period, Pierson had wisely taken the company in two directions, allowing the development of large long-range passenger-carrying aircraft and single-engine amphibians. The former saw the evolvement of the Vimy, and the latter the Viking amphibian, the Mk III version winning the 1920 Air Ministry competition for this type of aircraft. Supermarine was also competing in the 1920 competition; this company would become a subsidiary of Vickers in 1928, going on to produce aircraft such as Vickers-Supermarine, while always retaining its original identity.

Equipping the RAF far and wide, Vickers was always head and shoulders above other manufacturers in the field of long-range, load-carrying aircraft for the RAF. After the Vimy and its transport derivative, the Vernon, an aircraft of larger configuration appeared in 1924 in the shape of the Virginia. The latter went on to be the standard RAF night-fighter into the mid-1930s, while the bomber-transport version, the Victoria, served into the early stages of World War Two.

Another of Pierson's workmanlike designs was the Vulcan; a short-range single-engined airliner of, to be polite, tubby proportions. The aircraft was difficult to fly, and potential commercial sales never materialised. The Vimy Commercial was slightly more successful because of an order for 40 aircraft from the Chinese government, although how many of them were actually used is unknown. A similar number of Vickers Instructional Machines (VIMs), which were essentially redesigned F.E.2ds, were also supplied at the same time.

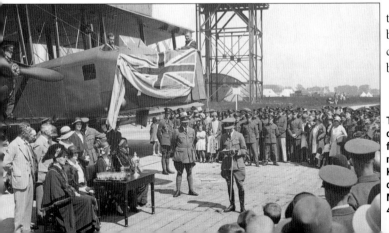

While the company continued to develop its big twin-engined bombers, transports and commercial aircraft, work was also being conducted on a new range of

The Vickers Virginia was the mainstay of the RAF's night-bomber force from the mid-1920s through to the mid-1930s. Here, a 500 (County of Kent) Squadron Virginia is being christened as the *Isle of Thanet* by the Mayors of Margate and Ramsgate on 4 June 1931.

metal-framed single-engined biplanes. The strength of World War One F.B.14's steel-tube airframe had been thoroughly tested at Farnborough in 1917, and now this method of construction was continued in 1923 with the Vixen. A derivative of the Vixen, the Venture, won an Air Ministry competition for a two-seat fighter reconnaissance aircraft, but only six were ever built for the RAF. Orders for the Vixen did come in from overseas in limited numbers, firstly from Chile in 1925 for 19 Mk Vs and then for 14 Valparaisos from Portugal, which also purchased a licence to build more.

The Vespa followed; an early example of a Short Take-off and Landing (STOL) aircraft, which was presented to the RAF as a general-purpose aircraft. Some sales came from Bolivia and Ireland, but the best publicity Vickers could wish for came about when Cyril Uwins flew a converted Vespa to 43,976ft in 1932, to capture the World Height Record.

Pioneering all-metal construction

Vickers formed a partnership with French aeronautical engineer Michel Wibault in 1925, a successful exponent of metal construction and its use in aircraft structures. Following the progress already made by Junkers since World War One, the Wibault technique, coupled with Vickers' ability to produce its own duralumin light alloy, resulted in several different types of aircraft during the 1920s and early 1930s. These included the Wibault Scout for Chile, the Vireo fleet fighter, the Viastra high-wing airliner and the Vellore and Vellox, both civilian aircraft, which took advantage of specialist Wibault sections such as corrugated fuselage panels.

As well as buying Supermarine in 1928, the heavy engineering interests of Vickers merged with Armstrong Whitworth, resulting in Vickers-Armstrongs Ltd. This merger did not include the aviation interests of Armstrong Whitworth, which remained independent as Sir W. G. Armstrong Whitworth Aircraft Ltd. Vickers' aircraft grew from strength to strength as Vickers-Supermarine, originally rivals, but now operating as one, with design and production departments working in close harmony. The first Vickers' aircraft to be built at the Supermarine works at Woolston, Southampton, was the Viastra Mk II, ordered for West Australian Airways. Virtually all of the wing structures for the Vildebeest were built at Woolston, as was the VIP Viastra, constructed especially for the Prince of Wales. On the other hand, Vickers at Weybridge found itself designing the wings for the Supermarine Southampton X flying-boat.

The period also saw an expansion and reorganisation of the Weybridge factory to accommodate large Air Ministry orders for Armstrong Whitworth Siskins, Hawker Harts and trainers, the latter being ordered at the beginning of the RAFs expansion scheme. Prior to this, Vickers still continued to design and build aircraft for the small commercial market, including the Vellore and the Vellox, the latter joining Imperial Airways. The Vellore, which was originally built for an Air Ministry specification, was to be the last complete aircraft constructed at the Crayford works. With regard to military orders, Vickers failed on two occasions to win the competition for a Virginia replacement during a period in the early 1930s when the disarmament philosophy was still prevalent; however, the rise of Hitler would change all that.

Enter Barnes Wallis

On 1 January 1930, following the demise of the R.100 airship, Barnes N. Wallis was appointed as chief designer (structures). In this role, Wallis, who had been an engineer since before World War One, began using the experience he had gained working with the R.100 to research how the strength/weight ratios of airframes could be improved. The result was the famous Wallis geodetic system of construction, which, incidentally, was not a method used in airships, but was a successful attempt to rid the structure of main members by employing latticework. Also worthy of note is that the Wibault stressed skin method was not employed in unison with the geodetic frame, and the more traditional fabric covering was used for much longer than by other aircraft manufacturers.

Wellesley and 'Wimpey'

Wallis' first aircraft was the M.1/30 torpedo-bomber of 1930, which was designed to operate from aircraft carriers. Wallis used his geodetic system in the aircraft to reduce weight, coupled with lightweight attachments for all tubular members and a smaller secondary structure. While it was indeed undoubtedly light for an aircraft of its size, Wallis may have gone a tad too far on this occasion, because the aircraft broke up on its maiden flight, forcing Capt J. 'Mutt' Summers and his flight test observer, J. Radcliffe, to take to their parachutes.

Next was the G.4/31, a specification which called for a general-purpose aircraft. Having already carried out experiments with a geodetic wing for the Viastra, as well as the fuselage, the G.4/31 used geodetics for the entire airframe. The effect on performance was dramatic, and the Air Ministry ordered the G.4/32 Monoplane, which was later christened as the Wellesley.

The excellent range and payload of the Wellesley saw the aircraft enter RAF service as a bomber rather than the intended general-purpose aircraft. The range was exploited by the RAF's Long-Range Flight, which captured the World Distance Record using Wellesleys in November 1937.

So as not to disrupt the geodetics of the Wellesley, the aircraft was forced to carry its weapon load within external pods rather than in a traditional bomb bay. The same problem occurred for specification B.9/32 for a new medium bomber, which was thankfully overcome; the aircraft, called the Wellington, went on to become the mainstay of early Bomber Command operations. The strength of the Wellington (nicknamed the 'Wimpy') may have been exaggerated a little over the years, but there is no doubt that many airmen have credited the geodetic design of the Wellington for their survival in the war.

In a shrewd move, the Wellington was built in government-sponsored shadow factories at Chester and Blackpool; both were relatively safe from air attack compared to Weybridge, which was severely hit by the Luftwaffe in September 1940.

Warwick and Windsor

A redesigned B.9/32, which was actually penned before the Wellington, was the larger Warwick. Hampered by slow development of its engines, the Warwick never enjoyed the success and long service of the Wellington.

Both Vickers and Supermarine tendered for the new four-engined bomber specification B.12/36, which was won by the latter and an order for two products was placed. This was Supermarine's first foray into this type of aircraft, and it would prove to be its last because a few weeks after Weybridge was hit, the Itchen works were also bombed, destroying all progress on the B.12/36. This seemed to fatefully level

Below left: The Wallis geodetic construction system is clearly visible in this group of part-built Vickers Wellingtons. It was initially criticised for being too complex for a semi-skilled labour force to handle, but this was far from the truth, and to prove the point, one particular bomber was constructed from start to finish in just 24 hours! (*Aeroplane*)

Below right: The Vickers (Aviation) Ltd factory on the eastern edge of the Brooklands race circuit, at Weybridge, in March 1938.

the playing field between the two companies; Supermarine would spend the war building the Spitfire while Vickers would build the Wellington.

Pierson did not give up on the idea of designing and building a large bomber for the RAF. A scheme was submitted to the Air Ministry for a giant six-engined bomber, crewed by seven and capable of carrying a 20-ton bomb load. Pierson's argument was two-fold: it was better to put seven aircrew at risk rather than a squadron's worth (on average 48), and that six engines were better than 24. The Air Ministry's reply was that a single bomber, rather than an entire squadron, would be more vulnerable and that multiple aircraft sent against a target would ensure that, even against the most defended targets, some would get through. Before the war was over, Pierson offered another giant bomber for Air Ministry approval, but this, once again, was dismissed.

One big bomber that did reach flight stage, if nothing else, was the B.3/42 Windsor, of which three prototypes were ordered as part of the aircraft's progressive development. The third prototype was fitted with a pair of remotely controlled barbettes behind each inner engine nacelle. The aircraft was promising when it first appeared, although its high speed caused the fabric to billow; this being cured with a new fabric with a metal-mesh woven into it. Intended to operate against the Japanese in the Pacific, large orders were initially placed, but with the end of World War Two these were quickly reduced before the entire project was cancelled in 1946.

Post-war commercial prosperity

Thanks to the developmental progress of the Wellington, Vickers was the first aircraft manufacturer to produce a post-war civilian airliner. The VC1 Viking, at first, even used the same geodetic construction technique for the wing and tail surfaces, while the fuselage was a metal monocoque with an unpressurised cabin. Later Vikings used stressed skin, which was first employed by Vickers on the Type 432 back in 1942. The Viking went on to serve in great numbers with BEA (British European Airways) during its early years and many airlines across the globe.

The next great success story for Vickers, and the British aircraft industry as a whole, was the VC2 Viscount. The Viscount was the first civilian aircraft to go into production with propeller-turbine power. The aircraft came about as one of the requirements of the Brabazon Committee, which set the path for all British-built civilian airliners. The Viscount broke no boundaries with regard to its construction, made from light-alloy and fitted with a single-spar wing, but this approach stood it in good stead for a number of decades, and no major problems ever beset the airliner during its commercial service. The Viscount's engine, the Rolls-Royce Dart, also set the standard for the world's turboprops, and derivatives of this powerplant still ply the skies today.

Valetta, Varsity and Valiant

Orders then began to come in from the RAF for a military version of Viking, which was eventually named the Valetta. The aircraft was employed successfully as a general-purpose transport, an army co-operation aircraft and a trainer. The successor to the Valetta was the Varsity, another long-serving aircraft, which fulfilled the RAF's multi-engine pilot, navigator and bomb-aimer training through to the mid-1970s.

The next huge military project was completed from design to flying prototype in just three years, which was remarkable considering that the aircraft was the complex B.9/48 Valiant. Designed with all-electric systems, the Valiant entered service in 1955, and the last of 104 built, thanks to well-organised sub-contracts, was delivered to the RAF in the autumn of 1958.

A big finale

While the work on the Valiant continued, the Viscount was being built at an average rate of three aircraft per week, mainly because production was aided by a new factory at Hurn, near Bournemouth.

Above left: Capt Joseph 'Mutt' Summers, CBE (right), was one of the great characters of the aviation world. He served as chief test pilot for both Vickers-Armstrongs and Supermarine and during his career carried out 54 prototype first flights and flew 366 different types of aircraft. He is with Capt Wakelin during early BEA Viscount proving trials at Kastrup, Copenhagen.

Above right: Gabe Robb 'Jock' Bryce, OBE, who joined Vickers-Armstrongs in 1947 as a test pilot under Mutt Summers, and took over as chief test pilot following Mutt's retirement. Bryce carried out several prototypes' maiden flights, including the VC10 on 29 June 1962. (*Aeroplane*)

The ability to not only design different aircraft simultaneously, but also build them simultaneously, was one of Vickers great strengths, which dated back to the period when the Siskins and Vildebeest could be constructed at the same time as the Virginia and Victoria.

Vickers did not rest on its laurels with the Viscount, and in response to the airline industry's requirements, the second-generation of turboprop airliners appeared in the shape of the Vanguard. Despite the Vanguard offering high-density seating and a huge underfloor freight capacity, the turbo-prop was finding it hard to compete with the pure jet, and sales of the aircraft suffered as a result. However, the 44 that were built gave excellent service with numerous owners until the mid-1990s; one of the last being flown into Brooklands in October 1996.

However, Vickers was ready for the jet revolution, and once again the company produced what is now seen as a classic, designed to a requirement by BOAC (British Overseas Airways Corporation). The arrival of the VC10 was slower than necessary because the Vickers V1000 project was also developing to a similar requirement, but the latter eventually fell by the wayside. Both popular with its crew and passengers alike, it was a tragedy that just 54 were built, but BOAC's stringent requirements contributed to the aircraft only appealing to a limited number of airlines, operating in certain conditions. Although the VC10 retired from civilian service in the early 1980s, the aircraft served the RAF as a transport/tanker faultlessly across the globe until its retirement in 2013.

The VC10 was the last aircraft to be prefixed with 'Vickers', because in 1960 the aircraft interests of the company were merged with Bristol, English Electric and Hunting Aircraft to form BAC (British Aircraft Corporation). While Supermarine was closed down in 1963, the Vickers name lived on until 1965, and Vickers-Armstrongs Ltd was not fully divested until 1977.

A beautiful aircraft from any angle, the prototype Vickers Type 1100 VC10, G-ARTA, at Brooklands in 1962. (*Aeroplane*)

Vickers Entry into Aviation

The rigid airships

H.M.A. No. 1 'Mayfly' (1911)

It was the rapid progress being achieved by the Germans in the field of airship development that finally prompted the Admiralty to propose a new giant airship for the Royal Navy in July 1908. The idea was written in a memorandum to the First Sea Lord, Adm Fisher, from Capt R. H. S. Bacon, who was the architect for the introduction of submarines into the Royal Navy in 1900. One of Bacon's recommendations was that the order should be placed with Vickers, Sons and Maxim for a rigid airship, the company already being closely associated with the Royal Navy, having built warships and supplied ordnance.

The idea was approved by the Admiralty and supported by the Prime Minister, H. H. Asquith, who recognised how useful an airship would be and was fully aware of how much investment the Germans had already made. By February 1909, the Committee of Imperial Defence signed off the idea and gave Vickers £30,000 for the task.

Design work began in late 1908 by a group of naval officers and Vickers' engineers within the confines of the Barrow-in-Furness naval construction yard. Technical knowledge was virtually non-existent at the time, with the designers only having the small luxury of some information leaked from Germany, and experience of building submarines. Construction work started on the airship in 1909 in a huge shed in the Cavendish Dock, as the plan was to float the machine out of its hangar on gondolas, in a similar fashion to the way the early Zeppelins were 'launched' on Lake Constance.

By now, the airship had been designated as the H.M.A. No. 1 and christened the 'Mayfly'. Construction continued through 1910, and during this time, the light alloy, duralumin, a German invention, became available. Vickers bought the rights to produce the metal, which ironically was not used in a Zeppelin until 1914. Construction of the Mayfly can only be described as proceeding on a trial-and-error basis, as many modifications were implemented at almost every stage of the build. A vast amount of research was conducted into the materials best suited for gasbags, the bulk of this work being fulfilled by Short Brothers. The Mayfly had a pair of control cars, or gondolas, which were made of Consuta as pioneered by S. E. Saunders of Cowes. The gondolas carried the airship's engines, two 160hp Wolseleys, the forward powerplant driving a pair of four-bladed wooden propellers and the rear a single two-bladed propeller.

Vickers' very first airship, H.M.A. No.1 Mayfly, in Cavendish Dock at Barrow-in-Furness during the airship's first successful outing from its giant floating hangar, which can be seen in the distance.

In September 1910, a full naval airship crew travelled from Portsmouth to Barrow aboard the light cruiser HMS *Hermione* in great secrecy. Throughout the winter, the crew trained on board the Mayfly, still inside its giant shed. On 22 May 1911, the Mayfly left its shed for the first time to carry out mooring trials using a 38ft-high mast mounted on a pontoon in Cavendish Dock. The airship spent two nights in the open in winds of up to 45mph before it was returned to its shed for further modifications. These revolved around reducing the airship's weight, which was too heavy by well over three tons. A great deal of naval type handling equipment was removed, such as an anchor, and several structural alterations were also made.

On 22 September, all of the work was completed, and all gas bags inflated; two days later, it was slowly moved from its shed again. However, just as the airship was clear of the shed, the 512ft-long Mayfly was hit by a sudden sharp wind, which pushed it over onto its beam ends. As it was slowly righted, the sound of cracking metal was heard, and the airship broke in two.

Following the subsequent enquiry, the First Lord of the Admiralty, Winston Churchill, did not allow the minutes of the report to be published. However, the general consensus at the time was that the severe squall caused the damage, while others later confessed that the airship was mishandled by the ground crews. The final cost of the H.M.A. No. 1 was believed to have been twice the £30,000 allocated, and Churchill, who at that time was not a fan of airships, was keen to draw a line under the proceedings.

H.M.A. No. 9 (1916)

Following the demise of the Mayfly, the Vickers airship department was closed down, but was revived again in 1913 following a request from the Admiralty for a new rigid airship, the H.M.A No. 9.

Designed by H. B. Pratt, who was being sub-contracted from S. E. Saunders, work began in April 1913. Under Pratt was a promising apprentice by the name of Barnes N. Wallis, who was originally apprenticed to the shipbuilders, J. Samuel White of Cowes. No. 9 was to be used as an experimental airship so that the Admiralty and the Defence Committee could decide whether or not any operational value would be gained from such a craft. It was ready for erection in August 1914 within a new large airship works, which had been constructed on the nearby Walney Island.

From this point on, No. 9 became a victim of politics, and in December 1914 a pair of Sea Lords declared that no more money should be 'wasted' on airships, which, unsurprisingly, was endorsed by Churchill. On 12 March 1915, Churchill ordered the cancellation of No. 9, but within two months he had moved to another government role, and by June the decision had been reversed. Time was now wasted recalling Vickers personnel and having to recondition the Walney plant.

Construction continued into 1916 because of regular design changes, problems with materials and the methods being used. Finally, on 16 November 1916, H.M.A. No. 9 became the first British-built rigid airship to fly, but it was initially unable to lift anywhere near the 3.1 tons it had been designed for. Later, two of its four 180hp Wolseley-Maybachs were replaced by a single 250hp Maybach taken from crashed Zeppelin L.33. Further modifications improved the airships lifting capacity to 3.8 tons, and on 4 April 1917, it was officially accepted by the Admiralty. The airship was later used for mooring trials and training at Howden in Yorkshire. Its service was short; No. 9 was damaged in a storm and broken up in 1918. Including the cost of the new factory at Walney, the entire No. 9 project had cost between £120,000 and £150,000.

H.M.A. No. 23 (1917) and R.26 (1918)

Once the Admiralty had approved the completion of H.M.A. No. 9 in June 1915, construction of a second 'sister ship' was agreed the following August. It was designated as the '23' class, in keeping with the running order of Royal Navy airships at the time.

Three '23' class airships were ordered in October 1915 to a similar design of the No. 9, but longer overall, with a more filled out bow and stern. No. 23 was to be built by Vickers, while No. 24 was built

The fateful moment on 24 September 1911, when a sudden strong gust caught the *Mayfly* as it was just clear of its shed. The airframe is beginning to twist and distort before the giant airship breaks in two.

by Beardmore and No. 25 by Armstrong Whitworth. Five more airships were ordered in January 1916, but only the first of them would be constructed by Vickers as the R.26, the 'R' signifying 'rigid'.

No. 23 was completed in October 1917 and the R.26 in March 1918; both were quickly entered into service flying North Sea patrols and used for training. In 1918, No. 23 was used for static tests with a pair of Sopwith Camels suspended underneath the keel, the concept being to launch the fighters in the air; the idea was continued with the Armstrong Whitworth R.33 in 1925.

Both No. 23 and the R.26 were good performers thanks to their 250hp Rolls-Royce Eagle engines, which pushed them along at over 50mph.

No. 23 (and R.26) had the honour of over-flying the German submarine fleet as it surrendered into Harwich in November 1918 and, in March the following year, was employed on a trial with a three-wire mooring system. With just 320 flying hours to its credit, No. 23 was withdrawn from use in September 1919.

Post-World War One, R.26 was also used for experimental duties, such as in early 1919 when it was used to test the viability of mooring such large airships out in the open. Its envelope eventually became rain-soaked, and it was later completely wrecked following a heavy snowstorm. With its gondolas removed, R.26 temporarily flew again, but its structure was so damaged the airship was written off for scrap on 10 March 1919.

R.80 (1920)

In 1916, Vickers found itself in a position where it could not accept orders for the new class of airship, which was based on information gleaned from the impressive Zeppelin L.33, captured in September. Vickers therefore suggested that it should design and build the biggest possible airship within the space available at Walney. The Admiralty accepted the proposal and an order for the R.80 was placed in November 1917.

Designed by Barnes Wallis, the R.80 was beautifully streamlined, rejecting all previous theories about what shape an airship should be. It now had much less drag than previous Vickers' designs and, combined with four 230hp Wolseley-Maybach engines, the R.80 could range up to 4,000 miles at 65mph and 6,400 miles at 50mph. The R.80 was also an effective military machine, equipped with a 2lb quick-firing gun and several .303in Lewis machine guns at various locations. The airship could also carry eight 230lb bombs stowed along the keel.

Completed in June 1920, the R.80 was first flown on 19 July, only to be damaged during a further test flight because it was not properly ballasted. Damage to the framework took until January 1921 to repair, when it was transferred to Howden as a crew training airship and then on to RNAS Pulham in Norfolk. Here, its structure was used for metal testing before this promising airship was dismantled in 1925, having flown for just 75 hours.

The non-rigid airships
The P.5, 6 and 7 (1917 and 1918)

In late 1912, an order was placed with Vickers from the Admiralty for a Parseval-type non-rigid airship of German design. Part of the contract involved Vickers entering a licence agreement with the owners of the Parseval patents, Luft-Fahrzeug Gesellschaft, on 25 November 1912. Vickers received a full set of drawings for the airship, a P.L.18 (Parseval No. 4), which was built at the Parseval works, Bitterfield, and delivered to the Admiralty at Farnborough in June 1913, having completed its maiden flight on 23 April. P.4 gave good service until it was withdrawn in July 1917.

By July 1913, Winston Churchill approved the purchase of a second Parseval from Germany, designated as the P.5, but in the end, it was actually built by Vickers at Barrow. The manufacture of two more Parsevals, the P.6 and P.7, were also approved; the envelopes of these being made in Germany.

In November 1913, Vickers, via Luft Fahrszeug, managed to negotiate a royalty-free deal from Motorenbau Gesellschaft for 20 Maybach engines for the sum of 120,000 Deutschmarks. As construction progressed with the three airships at Barrow, Vickers had trouble with the design of the control car structure and the transmission gear for the powerplant. The latter was subsequently dispensed with and swivelling propeller equipment, designed by Vickers, was put in its place. This resulted in the three airships being delayed until late 1917, and it was December before the flight trials were completed.

Little is known about the service of P.5, 6 and 7, but they were all employed on coastal patrol duties over the North Sea and off the east coast until the end of World War One.

R.100 (1929)

Following the end of World War One, several ideas promoting the airship as the only long-range air transport were put forward to the government. With an endurance of up to 24 hours, an airship could operate in all but the most serious of weather conditions and, at the time, no heavier-than-air machine could come close to it.

Vickers proposed a new transatlantic airship service all supported with designs and cost estimations backed by its experience with previous projects, including the R.80, which was still in use at the time. Apathy and official disinterest were the order of the day until a new scheme for a private passenger service to India and Australia was put forward. Cdr C. D. Burney was the driving force behind the idea, which would see all government airship material and stations taken over and financed by Vickers and the Shell Petroleum Group, but with an annual government subsidy. Not all points were agreed, but the government did start to realise that more efficient communication across the Empire was becoming important.

By 1924, a Labour government was in power and presented its own scheme for a service to India and Canada, all backed by Brig Gen Lord Thomson of Cardington. Two airships were subsequently ordered, the R.100 to be built by Vickers subsidiary, the Airship Guarantee Company (AGC), and the R.101, which would be built by the Royal Airship Works at Cardington.

Vickers was awarded the contract for the R.100 on 22 October 1924, for a fixed price of £350,000, with the caveat of a £1,000 fine for every half mile per hour that the finished article fell below the desired speed of 70mph. Terms of the contract also included that one flight should be made to Canada and back. Design was initially carried out at Vickers House from late 1924, but later moved to Crayford and concluded at the ex-RNAS Airship Station at Howden, which had been purchased by the AGC for £61,000.

The airship was designed by Barnes Wallis with a team that included chief calculator N. S. Norway (destined to become the famous novelist Neville Shute) and Maj P. L. Teed, an experienced metallurgist. Great effort was placed on producing the R.100 as simply and cheaply as possible, although Wallis still managed to include several novel features, such as a wire-mesh system of netting that stopped the gasbags from pressing against the longitudinal girders. This netting would germinate his idea for geodetic structures.

To make the airship as aerodynamic as possible, passenger accommodation was located within the hull of the ship in three decks, the lower one being used by the crew. A 56-seater dining saloon took up the entire centre deck and 40ft-long viewing promenades were located along each side of the airship. Cabins were provided for up to 100 passengers in two- and four-berth arrangements located on the centre and upper deck.

The R.100 was powered by six 670hp Condor IIIB engines, all mounted in tandem within three cars, driving a trio of three tractor and three pusher twin-bladed propellers. Kerosene-hydrogen engines were originally planned for the R.100, but the tried and tested Rolls-Royce unit was the wiser choice.

First flown from Howden on 16 December 1929, as G-FAAV, under the command of Maj G. H. Scott, the R.100 was being moored at Cardington just two hours later. Flight testing was conducted from the Bedfordshire station including a 54hr endurance flight; the majority of which was flown in fog, and a speed test that saw the airship achieving 81mph, much to the relief of the accountants. The airship carried out the required flight to Canada during July and August 1930, the R.100 taking 78hrs outbound, and thanks to good tail winds, 58hrs on the return leg.

The R.100 was criticised from many quarters regarding the strength and complexity of its construction, and even more so following the loss of the R.101 in October 1930. The loss of the latter, which also saw the deaths of several great supporters of long-distance airship operations such as Lord Thomson and Sir Sefton Brancker, the Director of Civil Aviation, would bring to an end any further ideas of the British-built airship. The R.100 was deflated at Cardington, while a decision was made about its future. Sadly, in November 1931, the decision was made to scrap the R.100, the framework of the mammoth airship was crushed flat by steamrollers and sold off for just £600.

The Vickers-built Blimps

Sea Scout (SS) Blimps

Nicknamed Blimps, Vickers built several SS-class airships at Barrow between 1915 and 1921. With a capacity of 70,000ft³ and 144ft long, the SS was flown by a crew of two, who operated from a BE type aircraft fuselage suspended by wire ropes below the envelope. With a range of 1,000 miles, the SS Blimps were very useful for carrying out patrols along the east coast of Britain and were also deployed across the Mediterranean.

Envelopes and gas bags for the SS and rigid airships were initially made at Barrow, but later in the war at a specialised centre at Douglas, on the Isle of Man. Rubber, which was originally imported from overseas, was also made by the Ico Rubber and Waterproofing Co Ltd, also a subsidiary of Vickers.

Completed in October 1917, H.M.A. No.23 was fitted with single control surfaces and remained in service until September 1919.

R.E.P. Type Monoplane No. 1, 3, 5, 7 and 8

Development

In early January 1911, Vickers, Sons and Maxim made the bold step of offering the Admiralty a new monoplane, which was, unlike anything else of the period, made of steel, with the exception of the wings. The high price of £1,500 may have been one of many factors that resulted in no interest from the Admiralty, but the fledgling company, which would become Vickers (Aviation) Ltd by the end of 1911, had already set itself apart from other aircraft manufacturers by daring to challenge established methods and techniques.

Design

The early monoplanes, of which only eight were built, were developments of a design by French aircraft designer Robert Esnault-Pelterie, and the first aircraft, No. 1, still incorporated some of his ideas in the rear fuselage. Vickers would also use Peterie's own aero engine, the R.E.P.

All of the R.E.P monoplanes featured a metal-tube airframe, which was the aircraft's most unique feature, giving it robustness over wooden-built machines.

No. 1 monoplane, a shoulder-wing aircraft with a deep slim fuselage, was constructed in the Vickers factory located at Erith in Kent. The manager of the Vickers aviation department was Capt Herbert F. Wood, who took No. 1 monoplane into the air for the first time in July 1911, from a brand-new aerodrome at Joyce Green, Kent.

Service

No. 1 was later flown from Brooklands, where the following year, the Vickers Flying School was established in new aircraft sheds along the Byfleet banking. No. 1 would subsequently be written off in an accident, while the following No. 2 monoplane was sold to Dr Douglas Mawson for the Australian Antarctic expedition of 1912. Damaged before the expedition began, the aircraft was still taken without its wings to be used as tractor sledge, but the engine oil froze in the extreme cold. Remarkably, the remains of this aircraft have been found in recent years where the expedition left it over 100 years ago.

The first five aircraft built were all very similar, although No. 5 had a deeper fuselage that gave the crew better protection from the weather. No. 6 saw the most extensive redesign and was entered for the Military Aeroplane Trials Competition in 1912. No. 6 had a much shorter wingspan, a 70hp Viale engine and side-by-side seating, the aircraft gaining the nickname the 'Vickers Sociable' because of it. The Viale engine proved to be unreliable and cost the monoplane any chance of doing well in the military competition.

No. 7 monoplane had a tandem seating arrangement and a more powerful 100hp Gnome engine fitted while the final machine, No. 8 was similar to No. 6 but had a Gnome engine fitted instead of the Viale.

Technical data – Monoplane Nos. 1–8	
ENGINE	(1, 2 & 3) One 60hp R.E.P (2 later fitted with 60hp Vickers-R.E.P); (6) One 70hp Viale (later fitted with 70hp Gnome); (7) One 100hp Gnome
WINGSPAN	(1, 2 & 3) 47ft 6in; (6 & 8) 35ft; (7) 34ft 6in
LENGTH	(1, 2 & 3) 36ft 5in; (7) 25ft
WING AREA	(1, 2 & 3) 290 sq ft; (6,7 & 8) 220 sq ft
EMPTY WEIGHT	(1, 2 & 3) 1,000lb; (7) 730lb
MAX SPEED	(1, 2 & 3) 56mph; (6) 63mph; (7) 70mph
RANGE	(7) 350 miles

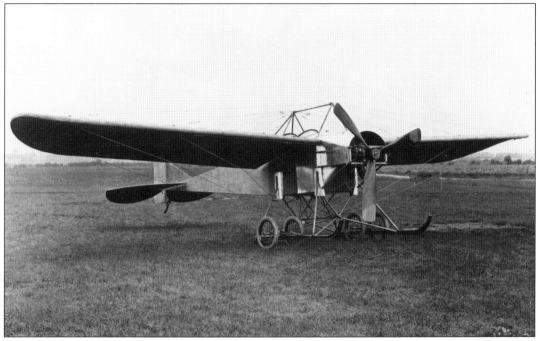

Vickers No.7 monoplane, complete with tandem seating, a twin-skid four-wheel undercarriage and power provided by a 100hp Gnome rotary engine.

No.1 monoplane pictured at Joyce Green, near Dartford, fitted with a fan-type REP engine.

E.F.B.1 'Destroyer', E.F.B.2 and 3

Development

Designed by George Henry Challenger and Archibald R. Low, the E.F.B.s (Experimental Fighting Biplane) were the first examples of aircraft specifically designed for an offensive role. The prototypes would lead to the successful 'Gunbus,' which would put Vickers firmly on the aircraft manufacturers' map.

Design

On 19 November 1912, a contract was issued to Vickers from the Admiralty for a fighting biplane armed with a machine gun. The Vickers design team quickly came to the conclusion that a pusher arrangement would be the most practical, with the air gunner in the nose of the aircraft. The aircraft was designated as the E.F.B.1 'Destroyer', the novel machine making its first public appearance at Olympia in February 1913.

The E.F.B.1 was an unequal-span biplane with the Wolseley engine mounted at the rear of a main nacelle, which accommodated the pilot and gunner. The tailplane was mounted on twin booms, which, like the nacelle structure and wing spars, were all made of steel. A single, belt-fed .303in Vickers-Maxim machine gun operated on a flexible mounting from the nose.

Service

The E.F.B.1 was received with great enthusiasm at Olympia, but the aircraft was still yet to fly. The date of the aircraft's first flight is unclear but is estimated to have been around March 1913 and its demise is also believed to have occurred on its maiden flight or certainly not long after.

However, the layout of the aircraft was clearly the way forward for Vickers and the same year the E.F.B.2 appeared. The aircraft had similar layout to its predecessor, once again with slightly unequal wings but with a nacelle fitted with large celluloid windows in an attempt to improve downward vision for both the pilot and gunner. The E.F.B.2 made its maiden flight in the hands of Vickers chief test pilot Harold Barnwell from Brooklands on 26 November 1913.

The E.F.B.3 continued the evolution; its main feature was ailerons, which replaced the wing-warping method of control used for the earlier aircraft. The belt-fed Vickers-Maxim, which had proved troublesome, was replaced by a drum-fed .303in Lewis machine-gun, a weapon which would remain in service into the 1940s.

Displayed at the Olympia Aero Show in 1914, the E.F.B.3 caught the attention of the Admiralty, which ordered six aircraft that were designated as the Vickers Type 30. However, such was the pace of design at the time that the Type 30 was superseded by a much later order for the E.F.B.5, which would be more familiarly known as the F.B.5 'Gunbus'.

The E.F.B.4, an advanced version of the 'Destroyer', was a design that never left the drawing board.

Technical data – E.F.B.1, 2 & 3	
ENGINE	(1) One 60/80hp Wolseley; (2 & 3) One 100hp Gnome Monosoupape
WINGSPAN	(1) 40ft; (2) 38ft 7in; (3) 37ft 4in
LENGTH	(1 & 3) 27ft 6in; (2) 29ft 2in
HEIGHT	(1) 11ft 11in; (2) 9ft 7in; (3) 9ft 9in
WING AREA	(1 & 3) 385 sq ft; (2) 380 sq ft
EMPTY WEIGHT	(1) 1,760lb; (2 & 3) 1,050lb
GROSS WEIGHT	(1) 2,660lb; (2) 1,760lb; (3) 1,680lb
MAX SPEED	(1) 70mph; (2 & 3) 60mph
RANGE	(2) 150 miles; (3) 300 miles
ENDURANCE	(1) 4½hrs

Above: First flown on 16 November 1913, the E.F.B.2 was the second link in the evolutionary chain that would lead to the successful Gunbus, an aircraft destined to see operational service over the trenches in Northern France.

Right: Pictured during its construction at Erith, the E.F.B.1 appeared complete at Olympia in February 1913, only weeks after this photograph was taken.

F.B.5 Gunbus, E.F.B.6 and F.B.9

Development

Having dropped the word 'Experimental' from its type listing, the results of Vickers' labour finally bore fruit with the F.B.5, which became the first aircraft specifically designed for aerial combat to become operational.

As covered in the previous section, the F.B.5 came about when the contract for six E.F.B.3s was taken over by the War Office. Further improvements in the design, such as a new forward nacelle and a rectangular tailplane, were made before the first of 224 built left the production line.

Service

Production of the F.B.5 Gunbus was carried out at the company's new Crayford works from late 1914, with the first machine flying on 17 July. The first three aircraft were delivered to 6 Squadron at Netheravon in November 1914, although two of these machines were relocated at Joyce Green to form the nucleus of the new Air Defence of London.

The Gunbus saw action for the first time on 25 December 1914, when 2nd Lt M. R. Chidson and his gunner, Cpl Martin, took off from Joyce Green to deal with a Taube monoplane, which is believed to have been shot down. Lt Chidson's aircraft was also the first F.B.5 to serve over the Western Front, the machine joining 2 Squadron at Merville on 7 February 1915.

The F.B.5 had its fair share of success against the enemy during its service but, like so many allied aircraft of the day, it was let down by an unreliable engine. One pilot, 2nd Lt G. S. M. Insall was awarded the VC for his actions on 7 November 1915, when he forced an Aviatik to land and then destroyed it with a single incendiary bomb as its crew attempted to open fire on the Gunbus.

One experimental development of the F.B.5 was the E.F.B.6, which was fitted with an increased upper wingspan in an effort to improve lift and the aircraft's load carrying capability.

The final variant of the Gunbus-type pushers was the F.B.9, which was modified to such a degree it was unofficially referred to as the 'Streamline Gunbus'. The F.B.9 looked a much tidier aircraft but only 95 were built, the majority going to training units. Several operational units are credited with having F.B.9s but only 11 Squadron, from May to July 1916, had them in any significant number.

Production

In total, 224 F.B.5s were built, 119 of them by Vickers at the Crayford works, 99 under licence by S A Darracq et Cie, Suresnes, France, and six by A/S Nielson and Winthers of Copenhagen, Denmark. The latter company also built 12 more aircraft as two-seaters. One E.F.B.6 was built by Vickers, while 95 F.B.9s were constructed by the company at Crayford (45) and Weybridge (50).

Technical data – F.B.5 & F.B.9	
ENGINE	One 100hp Gnome Monosoupape
WINGSPAN	(5) 36ft 6in; (9) 33ft 9in
LENGTH	(5) 27ft 2in; (9) 28ft 5½in
HEIGHT	(5) 11ft; (9) 11ft 6in
WING AREA	(5) 382 sq ft; (9) 340 sq ft
EMPTY WEIGHT	(5) 1,220lb; (9) 1,029lb
GROSS WEIGHT	(5) 2,050lb; (9) 1,820lb
MAX SPEED	(5) 70mph at 5,000ft; (9) 82.6mph at sea level
SERVICE CEILING	(5) 9,000ft; (9) 11,000ft
RANGE	250 miles

Right: The first of 224 Vickers F.B.5 Gunbuses built was No.664, which was one of six aircraft from War Office contract A2321, dated 18 December 1913. No.664 made its maiden flight on 17 July 1914.

Below: A very rare image of an F.B.5 built by A/S Nielson and Winthers of Copenhagen. Licensed to build six aircraft as standard F.B.5s with pilot and air gunner, a further licence for 12 aircraft to be built as two-seaters was also purchased. This is No.7, the first two-seater version of the F.B.5 ever built.

E.S.1 and E.S.1 Mk II 'Bullet'

Development

Most likely prompted by the complete lack of military aircraft available at the beginning of World War One, Vickers chief test pilot Harold Barnwell took it upon himself to design a single-seat scout-type aircraft of his own. Without gaining permission from the Vickers hierarchy, Barnwell designed and built the small aircraft, which became known as the 'Barnwell Bullet'. However, on its first flight, with Barnwell at the controls, the aircraft was a little difficult to handle and on landing the undercarriage collapsed causing the machine to end up on its nose. By this stage, the cat was out of the bag, but rather than sacking Barnwell on the spot, Vickers took his idea and gave the task of redesigning the aircraft to Rex K. Pierson.

Design

Pierson, who had learned to fly at the Vickers Flying School, redesigned Barnwell's creation into the E.S.1. Powered by a closely cowled Gnome Monosoupape, the tubby looking fighter expanded on the original aircraft by having larger tail surfaces and a stronger undercarriage. First flown in August 1915, the E.S.1 was sent to the Central Flying School (CFS) at Upavon for flight trials. Several deficiencies were pointed out, but these were rectified in a modified version designated as the E.S.1 Mk II, but also referred to as the E.S.2. This aircraft was fitted with an improved 110hp Clerget rotary and had a celluloid panel put into the top centre-section of the wing to improve visibility, which was one of the main criticisms of the CFS.

Two E.S.2s were built, one of them was employed to test the Vickers-Challenger machine gun synchronising gear, which enabled the weapon to be fired through a revolving propeller.

Service

One E.S.2 was sent to France in the summer of 1916, complete with a fixed, forward-firing, Vickers machine gun fitted with synchronising gear. The aircraft was received by 11 Squadron, then operating the F.B.5, for operational trials. Once again, though, the main problem with the E.S.2 was the number of blind spots, which was not good from a fighter pilot's point of view.

An E.S.2 was demonstrated in front of King George V in September 1915 during a visit to the Crayford factory and, later, the aircraft performed in front of a Russian Imperial aviation mission. The E.S.2 is also credited with being briefly trialled by 32 and 50 squadrons.

Technical data – E.S.1 & E.S.2	
ENGINE	(1) One 100hp Gnome Monosoupape; (2) One 110hp Clerget
WINGSPAN	(1) 24ft 4½in; (2) 24ft 5½in
LENGTH	20ft 3in
HEIGHT	8ft
WING AREA	215 sq ft
EMPTY WEIGHT	(1) 843lb; (2) 981lb
GROSS WEIGHT	(1) 1,295lb; (2) 1,502lb
MAX SPEED	(1) 114mph at 5,000ft; (2) 112.2mph at ground level
SERVICE CEILING	(2) 15,500ft
ENDURANCE	(1) 3hrs; (2) 2hrs at 8,000ft

Redesigned by R. K. Pierson from Harold Barnwell's original 'Barnwell Bullet', the E.S.1 was a lively performer but was let down by the pilot's poor view upwards and downwards.

E.F.B.7, 7A and 8

Development
Only days after the outbreak of World War One, Vickers employed pioneering aircraft designer Howard Flanders. He was tasked with designing a twin-engined military machine, which was capable of carrying a Vickers 1pdr (37mm) long recoil cannon. Flanders produced a development of his own single-engined Flanders B.2 biplane, which would be known as the E.F.B.7.

Design
The E.F.B.7 was made of a steel-tube structure covered in plywood and fabric with power provided by a pair of rotary Gnome Monosoupape engines, which were mounted between the unequal span wings. The position of the crew was where the initial design fell down, because the pilot was placed well behind the wings, while the gunner was isolated in the nose, too far away for effective communication. The gunner had a very roomy cockpit with an armoured floor and a rotating mount for the Vickers cannon.

The aircraft was later redesigned with the pilot brought forward of the wings and, because of a shortage of Gnome engines, a pair of lower-powered Renaults were fitted instead. Redesignated as the E.F.B.7A the aircraft was a poor performer because of the reduced horsepower available.

The next machine was the smaller E.F.B.8 designed by Rex Pierson, and rather than the cumbersome Vickers cannon, it was armed only with a single Lewis machine gun. Once again, the aircraft was not a huge success, as single-engined machines could carry the same armament and perform just as well.

This is the sole E.F.B.8 designed by Rex Pierson, which would lay the foundations for the Vickers Vimy. A Lewis machine gun can be seen fitted into the nose, and the Gnome engines are pictured with oil slinger rings around the radial engines.

Service

The E.F.B.7 was first flown in August 1915, which made it one of the world's first twin-engined military aircraft. The aircraft was handed over to the CFS for flight testing but a contract for 11 aircraft, to be built by Darracq & Co. Ltd of Townmead Road, Fulham, was cancelled on 16 February 1916.

The E.F.B.8 was a much better performer and when it made its maiden flight in November 1915; it was declared the fastest twin-engined aircraft at the time. As unsuccessful as both Experimental Fighting Biplanes were, Rex Pierson had sown the seeds for a much more celebrated aircraft. Within two years, the knowledge Pierson gained from the E.F.B.s would be used in the excellent Vickers Vimy.

Technical data – E.F.B 7 & 8	
ENGINE	Two 100hp Gnome Monosoupapes or two 80hp Renault V8s
WINGSPAN	(7 upper) 59ft 6in; (8 upper) 38ft 4in
LENGTH	(7) 36ft; (8) 28ft 2in
HEIGHT	(8) 9ft 10in
WING AREA	(7) 640 sq ft; (8) 468 sq ft
EMPTY WEIGHT	(7) 2,136lb; (8) 1,840lb
GROSS WEIGHT	(7) 3,196lb; (8) 2,610lb
MAX SPEED	(7) 75mph; (8) 98mph
CEILING	(7) 9,000ft; (8) 14,000ft
ENDURANCE	(7) 2½hrs; (8) 3hrs

F.B.12, A, B and C

Development
In 1914, Vickers enthusiastically joined with the Hart Engine Company with the hope that the latter's 150hp nine-cylinder radial engine would be produced in quantity to power the former's military aircraft. Unfortunately, it was much easier to build an aircraft at the time than produce a reliable aero engine in numbers and Hart was destined to fall by the wayside.

Design
Not dissimilar in appearance to a D.H.2 or F.E.8, the F.B.12 was constructed of wood with rounded-tip fabric-covered wings. The pilot was accommodated in a high-mounted nacelle, and a single fixed, forward-firing, .303in Lewis machine gun was fitted into the nose. The engine, which was initially meant to be a 150hp Hart, was mounted directly behind the pilot. However, the Hart engine was not ready and the F.B.12 was fitted with an 80hp Le Rhône when it made its maiden flight in June 1916.

Service
Obviously, the Le Rhône made the F.B.12 very underpowered, but after the fitment of a 100hp Gnome, the aircraft was redesignated as the F.B.12A. Even with the Gnome, the aircraft was 33 per cent down on its original design power, but in this configuration, the aircraft was sent to France in December 1916 for service trials. After operational trials, the only conclusion was that the F.B.12 was as good as the D.H.2 and F.E.8, both of which, by then, were becoming obsolete.

The 150hp Hart engine was ready for the F.B.12B, which first flew in early 1917. Prior to this, armed with the knowledge that the Hart engine was now ready for production, the War Office placed an order for 50 F.B.12Cs to be built by the Wells Aviation Company of Chelsea. Unfortunately for Hart, the F.B.12B crashed in February 1917, which resulted in the War Office cancelling the F.B.12C contract after just 18 were built. These aircraft were fitted with whatever rotary engine Wells Aviation could get hold of, which was generally a 110hp Le Rhône or a 100hp Anzani.

The F.B.12C was trialled by the RFC between May and July 1917, but with so few available and more modern types being developed, the aircraft fell by the wayside and only one HD (Home Defence) unit is believed to have operated the type for a short period.

Technical data – F.B.12	
ENGINE	(12) One 80hp Le Rhône; (A) One 100hp Gnome; (B) One 150hp Hart; (C) One 110hp Le Rhône or 100hp Anzani
WINGSPAN	26ft; (B upper) 29ft 9in
LENGTH	21ft 10in
HEIGHT	8ft 7in
WING AREA	(B) 237 sq ft
EMPTY WEIGHT	927lb
GROSS WEIGHT	1,447lb
MAX SPEED	87mph at 6,500ft
SERVICE CEILING	14,500ft
ENDURANCE	3¼hrs

The F.B.12 after being re-fitted with a 100hp Gnome Monosoupape engine.

F.B.11

Development

A War Office specification issued in early 1916 was quite a demanding one, considering military aircraft were still in their infancy. The specification called for an escort fighter powered by the very latest Rolls-Royce Eagle engine, which could not only provide bomber escort but could also be deployed as a Zeppelin destroyer.

Design

The aircraft would have to be large, with a three-man crew and a good arc of fire, not to mention that the machine must be capable of remaining airborne for up to seven hours during Zeppelin patrols. Designs were also tended by Armstrong Whitworth and Sopwith, while Vickers presented the F.B.11 designed by R. L. Howard-Flanders.

The F.B.11 was a big aircraft, a single-bay biplane with wings that spanned 51ft and power provided by a Rolls-Royce Eagle I, which gave 250hp. The pilot and one gunner were accommodated in traditional cockpits in the fuselage behind the trailing edge of the wing, while a second gunner was more precariously stationed in a nacelle mounted above and forward of the upper wing, called a 'fighting top'. Armament was a pair of .303in Lewis machine guns.

In comparison to the ungainly 'fighting top', the Eagle I engine was designed neatly into the fuselage, covered by an aerodynamic cowling, while the radiator was concealed within the fuselage directly behind it.

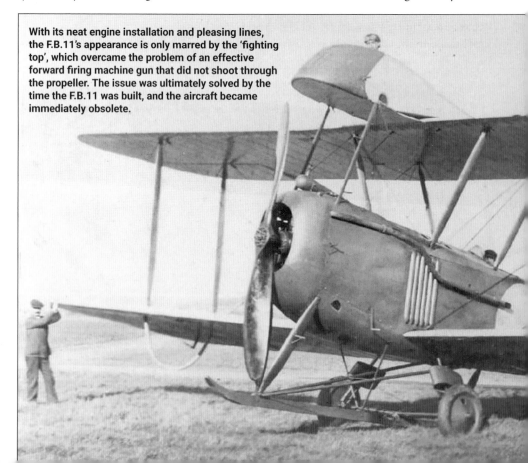

With its neat engine installation and pleasing lines, the F.B.11's appearance is only marred by the 'fighting top', which overcame the problem of an effective forward firing machine gun that did not shoot through the propeller. The issue was ultimately solved by the time the F.B.11 was built, and the aircraft became immediately obsolete.

Service

The first of two prototypes, ordered by the War Office, serialled A4814 and A4815, was first flown from Joyce Green in late September 1916. A4814 was then sent to RNAS Eastchurch for flight testing with the RNAS Design Flight in November 1916, but was later destroyed in an accident, which put Harold Barnwell in Crayford Hospital for over five weeks. A combination of a lack of power and poor lateral control were blamed for the accident and, without the second aircraft being completed, the concept was scrapped.

Technical data – F.B.11	
ENGINE	One 250hp Rolls-Royce Eagle I
WINGSPAN	51ft
LENGTH	43ft
HEIGHT	15ft
WING AREA	845 sq ft
EMPTY WEIGHT	3,340lb
GROSS WEIGHT	4,934lb
MAX SPEED	96mph at 5,000ft
SERVICE CEILING	11,500ft
ENDURANCE	4½hrs

F.B.14, A to H

Development

The next Howard-Flanders design was much smaller than the F.B.11, a conventional single-bay biplane with twin open cockpits, intended to be powered by a 230hp B.H.P. engine, which would evolve into the Siddeley Puma. Unfortunately for Vickers, and the F.B.14, the aircraft would have to make do with a powerplant that was 70hp down on what was needed to make this into a good aircraft.

Design

Although the F.B.14 was heavily influenced by Howard-Flanders, the fuselage still followed the proven steel-tube method of construction, which was first used in the early R.E.P. monoplanes. This method attracted official interest and the tubular design was thoroughly tested at Farnborough, yielding excellent strength qualities.

As the B.H.P. engine was not yet ready, a 160hp Beardmore was chosen instead, a powerplant that proved too unreliable and was replaced by a 120hp Beardmore instead. Once again, a well-designed Vickers aircraft had fallen foul of the lack of availability of the engine it needed.

Other engines did come along; the F.B.14A was fitted with a 150hp Lorraine-Dietrich, the F.B.14D had a useful 250hp Eagle IV, while the sole F.B.14F received a 140hp RAF4a air-cooled unit. F.B.14D C4547 was by far the most impressive of all built and during tests from Martlesham Heath the aircraft managed a speed of 115.5mph.

Service

It is not clear how many F.B.14s actually served with the RFC, but several are believed to have been sent to squadrons in the Middle East, while at least seven are credited with serving in HD squadrons.

F.B.14D C4547 was also modified for gunnery trials at Orfordness, the aircraft being fitted with one Vickers machine gun firing forwards, another at an angle of 45° and two more firing rearwards, one of them under the tail. On 22 July 1917, C4547, with Vernon Brown at the controls and Melville Jones (the inventor of the periscope gun sight) acting as gunner, became embroiled in an enemy raid while testing the gunsight. They engaged a Gotha bomber, which was driven back to the Belgian coast and was eventually shot down, crashing into the sea off Zeebrugge.

Production

There were 100 F.B.14s ordered and the serial range A678–A777 was allocated; in the end, only 50 of these were built, the majority delivered as airframes without engines. All were held in store at Islington before they were scrapped. A second order for 150 aircraft was allotted the serials A8341–A8490. The first 51 of this batch were built by Vickers at Weybridge but again placed in store at Islington until disposed of. One F.B.14, A3505, was fitted with a 160hp Beardmore; one F.B.14D was built, serialled C4547 (f/f March 1917) and one F.B.14 was converted to an F.B.14F and serialled A8391.

The F.B.14B (250hp Beardmore), F.B.14C (200hp B.H.P) and F.B.14G (350hp Lorraine) were all projects and never left the drawing board. An experimental civilian version, designated the F.B.14H, was also built circa 1919 but never flew.

Technical data – F.B.14 & 14D	
ENGINE	(14) One 160hp Beardmore; (14D) One 250hp Rolls-Royce Eagle IV
WINGSPAN	(14 upper) 39ft 6in; (14D upper) 42ft
LENGTH	(14) 28ft 5in; (14D) 30ft 8in
HEIGHT	(14) 10ft; (14D) 10ft 3in
WING AREA	(14) 427 sq ft; (14D) 485 sq ft
EMPTY WEIGHT	(14) 1,662lb; (14D) 2,289lb
GROSS WEIGHT	(14) 2,603lb; (14D) 3,308lb
MAX SPEED	(14) 99.5mph at ground level; (14D) 111.5mph at 6,500ft
SERVICE CEILING	(14) 10,000ft; (14D) 15,500ft
ENDURANCE	(14) 3¾hrs; (14D) 3½hrs

F.B.14 A3505, which was built out of sequence from the two main production batches, but was still powered by a standard 160hp Beardmore.

F.B.16A, D, E and H

Development

The F.B.16 was the next in a series of fighters designed by Rex Pierson, which were intended to make use of the Hart radial engine. Once again though, the Vickers-sponsored powerplant proved to be disappointing, but an alternative was found and the F.B.16 showed great promise as a result.

Design

Working around the Hart engine, Pierson redesigned the aircraft into the F.B.16A, which was powered by a 150hp Hispano Suiza. The French-designed powerplant was water-cooled but was proving increasingly popular with British aircraft manufacturers. Both the F.B.16B and 'C' never left the drawing board, the former was intended to be powered by a 200hp Hispano Suiza and the latter a 200hp Lorraine.

The F.B.16D was by far the most promising of all, the little fighter being fitted with a 200hp Hispano Suiza engine. The tubby little 'D' was a great performer, and it also featured a novel method of firing its machine guns, which involved a single Lewis mounted between the vee of the cylinder blocks of the engine, firing through a hollow propeller shaft.

The final variant was the 275hp Lorraine-Dietrich powered F.B.16E, which was intended for massed production by S A Darracq in France. Built under licence, the 'E' had larger twin-bay wings to compensate for the heavier engine, but large-scale production never materialised.

Service

While no F.B.16s ever entered RFC service, the F.B.16D certainly caught the attention of Maj James B. McCudden, who was a regular visitor to Joyce Green whilst on leave from fighting over the trenches in France. Taken from his memoirs, the air ace spoke fondly of the F.B.16D as follows:

On June 22, 1917, I flew a little Vickers tractor, the F.B.16D, which was now fitted with a 200hp Wolseley-Hispano. I climbed to 10,000ft in eight minutes and at that height the machine did 136mph. Whilst flying that machine I got some idea of the speed of future machines, for at 10,000ft it was 30mph faster at least than anything I had yet flown. Harold Barnwell liked this little machine, although he said it cost him a new pair of trousers every time he flew it, as it always smothered his legs in oil. It had a very deep fuselage rather out of proportion to the size of the machine and Barnwell always alluded to it as the 'Pot-Belly'.

McCudden wanted to take the F.B.16D to France with him but the policy of the day was that personal aircraft were not allowed if not already serving as standard equipment.

Production

Before the F.B.16D could enter mass production, orders had already been placed for large numbers of S.E.5As, many of which would be built by Vickers at Crayford and Weybridge. One F.B.16 was built, together with a few F.B.16As (the second aircraft was serialled A8963) and one F.B.16D, which was a conversion of A8963. The French built only one F.B.16E. Designated as Vic 16.C1, it crashed on 29 July 1918.

Technical data – F.B.16A & D	
ENGINE	(A) One 150hp Hispano Suiza; (D) One 200hp Hispano Suiza; (E) One 275hp Lorraine-Dietrich 8 Bd
WINGSPAN	(upper) 25ft; (E) 31ft
LENGTH	19ft 6in
HEIGHT	8ft 9in
WING AREA	207 sq ft
EMPTY WEIGHT	1,376lb
GROSS WEIGHT	1,875lb
MAX SPEED	135mph at 10,000ft
SERVICE CEILING	18,500ft
ENDURANCE	2¼hrs

Nicknamed the 'Pot-Belly' by Harold Barnwell, F.B.16D A8963 was also a particular favourite of Capt James McCudden, who is pictured by the tubby fighter.

F.B.19 Bullet Mk I and Mk II

Development
The F.B.19 was a developed version of the E.S.1 and 2, which first appeared in August 1916. The fighter came in two versions, the Mk I with un-staggered wings and Mk II with staggered.

Design
Designed by George Henry Challenger, an order was first placed by the War Office for the F.B.19 in the spring of 1916. The aircraft featured the designer's own Vickers-Challenger synchronised interrupter gear for a single Vickers machine gun. The Mk I version could be fitted with either a Gnome or Le Rhône rotary piston engine, while the Mk II was equally flexible and could be powered by either a Clerget or Le Rhône.

Service
At least 36 F.B.19 Mk Is were used by RFC squadrons and approximately half a dozen were sent to France for evaluation, but the majority were despatched to Palestine and Macedonia. A dozen Mk IIs served across the Middle East with 50 and 111 squadrons in Palestine and 11, 17 and 47 squadrons in Macedonia.

A single Mk I was sent to Russia as a demonstration aircraft and, as a result, an order for 12 further Mk Is was placed, these being shipped to Archangel in 1917. The aircraft were intended for service with the Imperial Russian Air Service, but none were used. The Russian Revolution then intervened, and several remained in crates on the dockside, until they were destroyed by the Royal Navy in 1919. The handful that was assembled saw brief service with the Bolshevik forces.

Production
In total, 53 F.B.19 Mk Is were ordered under contract 87/A/536 in September 1916, although the only known serials are A2992–A2122. Twelve F.B.19 Mk IIs were built under contract 87/A/1345 in December 1916 and serialled 5225–5236. All of these aircraft were built at Weybridge.

Technical data – F.B.19 Bullet Mk I & II	
ENGINE	(I) One 110hp Gnome Monosoupape or One 110hp Le Rhône; (II) One 110hp Le Rhône or One 110hp Clerget
WINGSPAN	24ft
LENGTH	18ft 2in
HEIGHT	8ft 3in
WING AREA	215 sq ft
EMPTY WEIGHT	(I) 900lb; (II) 890lb
GROSS WEIGHT	(I) 1,485lb; (II) 1,475lb
MAX SPEED	(I) 102mph at 10,000ft; (II) 98mph at 10,000ft
SERVICE CEILING	(I) 15,000ft; (II absolute) 16,500ft
ENDURANCE	(I) 2¾hrs; (II) 3hrs

An unknown Russian pilot poses next to a Vickers F.B.19 Mk I '6', which may have been during the brief period the type was used by the Bolsheviks after the October Revolution phase of the Russian Revolution of 1917.

F.B.24A, B, C, D, E and G

Development
The F.B.24 was the third and final design to leave the Vickers stable that was intended to be fitted with the ill-fated Hart radial engine. The aircraft pushed no boundaries in design and was meant to be operated in the two-seat fighter-bomber reconnaissance role, in a similar vein to the Bristol F.2B fighter.

Design
Designed by Harold Barnwell's brother Frank, who would later be better known for his design work with the Bristol Aeroplane Company, the F.B.24 was found to be lacking an engine before the prototype was completed in December 1916. Eventually, the 150hp Hispano-Suiza 8 engine was used for both prototypes, designated the F.B.24A and the F.B.24B respectively. It is not clear if just the 'A' was later converted to a more powerful 200hp Hispano-Suiza, but the conversion resulted in the F.B.24D. The F.B.24A first flew in March 1917.

The twin-bay biplane had a rectangular shaped fuselage and the pilot and the observer/air gunner had separate cockpits, but these were located very close together. The pilot was positioned directly under the upper wing and, despite the fitment of a pair of transparent panels, the same old problem of poor visibility, which had plagued earlier Vickers' designs, continued with the F.B.24. Armament for all F.B.24s was one fixed Vickers machine gun and one moveable Lewis machine gun.

The F.B.24C was fitted with a 275hp Lorraine-Dietrich 8Bd engine, which was a water-cooled V8. This engine was fitted by S A Darracq, but its bulky design did nothing to improve the pilot's view.

Vickers claimed that the F.B.24C had a promising performance, but after flight testing by the French, the aircraft was found to be performing far below the manufacturer's performance figures and was not taken on for military service.

The 200hp Hispano-Suiza or Wolseley Viper-powered F.B.24E was a radical attempt to improve the pilot's view by raising the position of the fuselage so that it was in line with the upper wing. The final version was the F.B.24G, which was similar in appearance to the 'E' but was powered by a 375hp Lorraine-Dietrich engine. The V-12 engine was installed by S A Darracq but did not fly until 26 May 1919.

Technical data – F.B.24	
ENGINE	(A & B) One 150hp Hispano-Suiza 8; (C) One 275hp Lorraine Dietrich 8Bd; (D) One 200hp Hispano-Suiza; (E) One 200hp Hispano-Suiza or Wolseley Viper; (G) One 375hp Lorraine Dietrich V-12
WINGSPAN	(C) (upper) 37ft 6in; (E) (upper) 35ft 6in
LENGTH	(C) 26ft 6in; (E) 26ft
WING AREA	(C) 384 sq ft; (E) 340 sq ft
EMPTY WEIGHT	(C) 1,709lb; (E) 1,630lb
GROSS WEIGHT	(C) 2,650lb; (E) 2,610lb
MAX SPEED	(C) 129.5mph at 10,000ft; (E) 122mph at 5,000ft
ABSOLUTE CEILING	(C) 23,000ft; (E) 16,000ft
ENDURANCE	(C & E) 3hrs

The only F.B.24C to be fitted with a 275hp Lorraine-Dietrich engine by S. A. Darracq, based in Suresnes, France.

F.B.23 and F.B.25

Development

A planned development of the F.B.9 Gunbus failed to materialise in the F.B.23, which was also a pusher fighter designed with a span of 38ft. However, a version capable of carrying a Crayford rocket gun did appear in the form of the F.B.25, which was constructed in Vickers own experimental workshop at Gravel Hill, Bexleyheath.

Design

Even though the F.B.23 never left the drawing board, three different variants were proposed, starting with the original aircraft powered by a 150hp Salmson, the F.B.23A by a 150hp Hart and the F.B.23B by a 200hp Hispano-Suiza 8 engine.

A twin-bay biplane with equal-span un-staggered wings, the F.B.25 had several novel features, including one of the earliest attempts to accommodate the crew in a side-by-side arrangement, rather than the more traditional tandem. This was almost achieved in the aircraft's wider than usual nacelle, with the gunner's position set slightly forward and to the right of the pilot. Armament was a single Vickers-Crayford rocket gun (aka a Vickers Q.F. Gun Mk II) which fired 40mm (1.59in) shells, not rockets.

Another unusual feature of the F.B.25 was its undercarriage, which was an oleo-pneumatic design. The design of the F.B.25 was pushed and pulled in many different ways, with one proposal involving the fitment of a small searchlight in the nose of the aircraft for night operations. Another idea was to add a small nose wheel to stop the aircraft turning over on landing, which was a common problem with many night-fighting machines.

Power was to be provided by a 200hp Hispano-Suiza 8, but as the design evolved and the weight reduced, and because of the lack of searchlight and nose wheel, a 150hp Hispano-Suiza was found to be sufficient, which was just as well as the 200hp was not yet available.

Service

Only one F.B.25 was ever built, and this was first flown in spring 1917. Early flight testing by Vickers was not encouraging, the aircraft's general handling proving to be rather poor. Regardless, the aircraft was sent to Martlesham Heath in June 1917 for military trials where, unsurprisingly, the early Vickers' test reports were endorsed by service test pilots. Flight controls were criticised, and the aircraft was particularly difficult to handle when the Hispano-Suiza was turned off. The F.B.25 was also described as 'unmanageable' in winds greater than 20mph, making the aircraft completely unsuitable for night operations, let alone day time ones.

No production order was placed for the F.B.25 and, in July 1917, the sole example was wrecked at Martlesham Heath by a service test pilot.

Technical data – F.B.25	
ENGINE	One 150hp Hispano-Suiza
WINGSPAN	41ft 6in
LENGTH	28ft 1in
HEIGHT	10ft 10in
WING AREA	500 sq ft
EMPTY WEIGHT	1,608lb
GROSS WEIGHT	2,454lb
MAX SPEED	86mph at 5,000ft
SERVICE CEILING	11,500ft
ENDURANCE	4½hrs

The two-seater F.B.25 night-fighter, pictured in 1917 after it was fitted with an oleo-pneumatic undercarriage and a Vickers-Crayford rocket gun.

F.B.26 Vampire Mk I and F.B.26A Vampire Mk II

Development

Much more sophisticated than the F.B.12, the F.B.26 was one of the last of the line of single-seat pusher biplane fighters, constructed by Vickers during World War One. The aircraft would ultimately miss out to the Sopwith Salamander, but the advanced thinking that the aircraft created was utilised many years later in the Vickers COW gun fighter, which did not emerge until 1931.

Design

A development of the F.B.12, this aircraft, which was also known as the Vampire Mk I, was a twin-bay biplane with a nacelle, which was high-mounted just for the pilot. The original armament was a pair of .303in Lewis machine guns and power was provided by a 200hp Hispano-Suiza, mounted at the rear of the nacelle, driving a four-blade propeller.

Two F.B.26s, B1484 and B1486, were fitted with Eeman three-gun universal mountings, which gave an angle of fire up to 45° and were specifically designed for attacking enemy bombers from below. Both these aircraft also incorporated a few modifications, such as a repositioned radiator and redesigned wing structure, before they were evaluated at Martlesham Heath.

B1485 was converted to become the only F.B.26A Vampire Mk II (aka the 'Trench Strafer'), the main difference being a 230hp Bentley engine and an armoured nacelle, as the aircraft was meant to be employed in the ground-attack role.

Service

The un-serialled prototype was first flown by Harold Barnwell in May 1917, but it was destined to be lost during an evening test flight on 25 August 1917. Having just taken off from Joyce Green, Barnwell was seen to inexplicably spin into the ground directly in front of his loyal mechanic, H. K. Kingsnorth, who was the only witness to the fatal accident.

The second of just three further aircraft, B1484 was the only Vampire to be tested by the RFC, beginning with 39 Squadron and then 141 Squadron in February 1918. Declared unsuitable for Home Defence duties, a potential use as a close air support aircraft was suggested, which resulted in the one and only Vampire Mk II.

Production

One prototype (powered by a 200hp Hispano-Suiza) plus a production order for six aircraft, B1484–B1489, were ordered as Vampire Mk Is under contract AS27055/1 on 19 September 1917. However, only three of this order would actually be built. B1485 was later converted with a 230hp Bentley B.R.2 and was redesignated as the F.B.26A Vampire Mk II.

Technical data – F.B.26 Vampire Mk I & F.B.26A Vampire Mk II	
ENGINE	(I) One 200hp Hispano-Suiza; (II) One 230hp Bentley B.R.2
WINGSPAN	(upper) 31ft 6in
LENGTH	(I) 23ft 5in; (II) 22ft 11in
HEIGHT	9ft 5in
WING AREA	267 sq ft
EMPTY WEIGHT	(I) 1,470lb; (II) 1,870lb
GROSS WEIGHT	(I) 2,030lb; (II) 2,438lb
MAX SPEED	121mph at 5,000ft
SERVICE CEILING	(I) 20,500ft; (II absolute) 19,000ft
ENDURANCE	(I) 3hrs; (II) 2hrs

The first F.B.26 Vampire Mk I, B1484, from a production order for just six aircraft, of which only three were ever completed. The aircraft is pictured after being modified with an Eeman three-gun universal mounting with a trio of .303in Lewis machine guns.

Vimy (F.B.27), Vimy Mk II (F.B.27A) and Commercial

Development

The excellent Vimy had its roots in the E.F.B.7 and 8 twin-engined fighters of late 1915; their general layout, and the experience gained at the time, proved to be very useful to Rex Pierson when the Air Board made a request to Vickers for a new twin-engined bomber in 1917.

Design

Having drawn up the general design of the iconic Vimy (known as the F.B.27 until 1918) on a piece of foolscap paper in the Air Board's HQ, the Hotel Cecil, in July 1917, Rex Pierson set to work and, on 16 August 1917, a contract for three prototypes was placed. The main criterion for the aircraft was that it should be capable of carrying out long-range operations at night against targets in Germany.

Owing to a shortage of suitable engines the first three aircraft, B9952–B9954, were powered by the 200hp Hispano-Suiza, 260hp Salmson, 260hp Sunbeam Maori and 300hp Fiat A-12. A fourth prototype, F9569, was powered by the reliable Rolls-Royce Eagle VIII, which would later be used in the production machine. The latter was unofficially designated as the F.B.27 Mk IV, but once the aircraft entered production it was known as the Vimy Mk II.

Two of the prototypes were lost through engine failures, while the Eagle-powered machine, which was delivered to Martlesham Heath on 11 October 1918, proved the soundness of the design. With an average speed of 100mph and an endurance of 11hrs, the Vimy was armed with two .303in Lewis machines guns, one in the nose and one aft of the wings, and could carry a bomb load of 2,476lb; a figure that was not dramatically surpassed at the beginning of World War Two.

A civilian version of the aircraft, called the Vimy Commercial, was built with a large diameter fuselage, the first aircraft flying from Joyce Green on 13 April 1919, in the hands of Stan Cockerell. Of those built, 40 were sent to China, but only seven of them ever flew. The Vimy Commercial would later serve the RAF as the Vernon and five were converted as ambulances. Civil versions of the standard Vimy included the most famous of all, which was flown across the Atlantic by Alcock and Brown in June 1919.

Service

The prototype Vimy was first flown from Joyce Green by Gordon Bell on 30 November 1917, and it entered service with the RAF's Independent Air Force in October 1918. Only three were in service before they could be fully deployed operationally prior to the Armistice being signed. Before the war ended, there were 1,130 Vimys on Vickers' order books, but this number was dramatically reduced and all production was later centred at Weybridge.

The Vimy was not fully operational with the RAF until July 1919 but remained in the front line until 1925, when the Virginia began to take over. 502 Squadron was the last significant unit to fly the type until 1929, although a few were retained for training duties as late as 1938.

Production

Originally 1,130 Vimys were ordered under 18 different contracts from March 1918, but the majority of these were cancelled at the end of World War One. It is believed that 232 were actually built, including four prototypes. There were six civil Vimys and 44 Vimy Commercials, the bulk of these being ordered for China. Five Vimy ambulances were also built at a cost of £6,500 each, all of them being employed in the Middle East.

Technical data – Vimy, Vimy Mk II & Commercial	
ENGINE	Two 200hp Hispano-Suizas; (II & C) Two 360hp Rolls-Royce Eagle VIIIs
WINGSPAN	67ft 2in; (II & C) 68ft
LENGTH	43ft 6½in; (C) 42ft 8in
HEIGHT	15ft 3in; (II & C) 15ft 7½ in
WING AREA	1,326 sq ft; (II & C) 1,330 sq ft
EMPTY WEIGHT	5,420lb; (II) 7,101lb; (C) 7,790lb
GROSS WEIGHT	9,120lb; (II & C) 12,500lb
MAX SPEED	87mph at 5,000ft; (II) 103mph at ground level; (C) 98mph at ground level
SERVICE CEILING	6,500ft; (II) 7,000ft; (C absolute) 10,500ft
ENDURANCE	3½hrs; (II) 11hrs
RANGE	(C) 450 miles

The fourth and final F.B.27 prototype (Mk IV), F9569, fitted with a pair of Rolls-Royce Eagle VIII engines. It was these engines that proved by far to be the most reliable tested to date and would secure the future of the aircraft.

Above left: Vimy F8642 was one of 50 aircraft originally ordered in 1918 under contract 35A/1257/C1166. The bomber is pictured climbing out of Brooklands in April 1926.

Above right: In February 1920, the intrepid Lt Col P. van Ryneveld and Mjr Q. Brand attempted the first flight from London to South Africa. Their aircraft, pictured here at Brooklands prior to the flight, was G-UABA, named the *Silver Queen*. Unfortunately, the aircraft was wrecked 80 miles from Wadi Halfa. The flight was continued in a second Vimy named *Silver Queen II* and finally in a South African Air Force DH.9.

Viking I, II, III, IV and V, Vulture (VI) and Vanellus (VII)

Development

The Viking family was a successful series of amphibians, the development of which began in December 1918. Destined to be the one and only Viking I, the prototype, G-EAOV, was a twin-bay, five-seat cabin biplane powered by a single 275hp Rolls-Royce Falcon engine.

Design

Constructed at Weybridge, the Viking I was first flown from Brooklands by Vickers' chief test pilot Sir John Alcock in November 1919. Sadly, on 18 December, the Viking crashed in fog near Rouen and Alcock was killed.

The slightly modified Viking II followed in 1919, powered by the ubiquitous Rolls-Royce Eagle VIII. The 360hp engine was mounted independently from the wing and was mounted on a pylon. The aircraft also had larger wheels, a bigger wing area and an extra rudder fitted behind the centrally mounted fin. First flown by Vickers' new chief test pilot, Stan Cockerell, the aircraft was registered as G-EASC in June 1920 and, by August, had won the Antwerp Seaplane Trials.

The Viking III followed, modified still further, mainly in response to Cockerell's extensive report on the Mk II. The main difference between the two aircraft was another power increase for the Mk III in the shape of a 450hp Napier Lion engine. Registered as G-EAUK, the Viking III was entered into the Air Ministry Competition for civil aircraft which was held at Martlesham Heath and Felixstowe in September and October 1920. The Viking III won the competition by a whisker over the Supermarine Commercial Amphibian to take the £10,000 prize. Thanks to the high public profile achieved in this competition, commercial interest began to grow ready for the next variant.

Production

A solid production line was finally in place at Weybridge for the Viking IV, which featured a host of modifications and refinements gained from experience with the first three designs. The Viking IV was by far the most successful of the breed; 21 of the 31 Vikings sold were Mk IVs.

Only two Vikings were classified as Mk Vs, N156 and N157, and both were supplied with special equipment for use by the RAF in Iraq. The Viking VI, aka the Vulture I, was next in line, powered by a 450hp Napier Lion. Only two were built, and the second aircraft was powered by a 360hp Eagle IX and was designated as the Vulture II. Both Vultures were used for an attempt on an around the world flight in 1924, but unfortunately neither aircraft came close to achieving it.

The final member of the Viking family was the Mk VII, named Vanellus, ordered by the Air Ministry to specification 46/22 for a three-seat fleet spotter; a single aircraft, N169, was built.

Technical data – Viking I, III, IV & Vulture (VI)	
ENGINE	(I) One 270hp Rolls-Royce Falcon III; (III, IV Type 55 & VI) One 450hp Napier Lion; (IV Type 69) One 360hp Rolls-Royce Eagle IX
WINGSPAN	(I) 37ft; (III) 46ft; (IV) 50ft; (VI) 49ft
LENGTH	(I) 30ft; (III) 32ft; (IV Type 55) 34ft 2in; (IV Type 69) 34ft; (VI) 38ft 2in
HEIGHT	(I & III) 13ft; (IV Type 55) 14ft; (IV Type 69) 14ft 2in; (VI) 14ft 6in
WING AREA	(I) 368 sq ft; (III) 585 sq ft; (IV) 635 sq ft; (VI) 828 sq ft
EMPTY WEIGHT	(I) 2,030lb; (III) 2,740lb; (IV Type 55) 4,040lb; (IV Type 69) 4,020lb; (VI) 4,530lb
GROSS WEIGHT	(I) 3,600lb; (III) 4,545lb; (IV Type 55) 5,790lb; (IV Type 69) 5,650lb; (VI) 6,500lb
MAX SPEED	(sea level): (I) 104mph; (III) 110mph; (IV Type 55) 113mph; (IV Type 69) 100mph; (VI) 98mph
RANGE	(I) 340 miles at 80mph; (III) 420 miles at 90mph; (IV Type 55) 925 miles with long-range tanks

Above: **Viking IV G-EBED was flown by Capt Leslie Hamilton, who used the amphibian as an air taxi between Lowenstein and St Moritz winter sports centre in Switzerland. Hamilton would land on soft snow and take off, with the wheels down, from hard snow or ice.**

Right: **G-CAEB was the only civilian Viking IV operated in Canada, initially by Laurentide Air Service. The aircraft enjoyed a long and varied service until September 1932, when a fuel line broke in flight. The pilot made a good forced landing in the Strait of Georgia and, along with his passengers, managed to escape before the Viking was destroyed by fire.**

VIM 'School Machine'

Development

The VIM was part of an order from the Chinese government that was placed in 1919. As well as 35 VIMs, the order also included 40 Vimy Commercials and 20 reconditioned Avro 504Ks. The plan was to establish a civilian aviation foothold in China, but the country's unstable political situation meant that the proposal was a failure.

Design

The VIM was actually constructed from surplus components from the Royal Aircraft Factory F.E.2ds. Vickers modified the nacelle of the aircraft to accommodate a pupil in the front cockpit and the instructor in a rear cockpit.

Power was provided by a war-surplus 360hp Rolls-Royce Eagle VIII engine, purchased from the Aircraft Disposal Company (ADC), giving the VIM good performance for a training biplane. The fitting of the Eagle VIII was calculated, as the aircraft could double as a ground maintenance trainer for ground crew working on the Vimy Commercial, as well as doubling as an advanced trainer, once student pilots had mastered the 504K. The cockpits were also arranged for future Vimy Commercial pilots, the instrumentation and layout being very similar to the larger twin-engined machine.

Service

It is not clear how much use was made of the VIM in China, but if the use of the Vimy Commercials is anything to go by, it is quite possible that very few actually left their crates after arriving in the country.

Production

In total, 35 VIMs were built, all of which were supplied to China.

Technical data – VIM	
ENGINE	One 360hp Rolls-Royce Eagle VIII
WINGSPAN	47ft 8in
LENGTH	32ft 4in
EMPTY WEIGHT	2,950lb
LOADED WEIGHT	3,645lb
MAX SPEED	100mph
CEILING	13,000ft
ENDURANCE	2¾ hrs

Basically a rebuilt version of the RAF F.E.2D, the VIM differed by being powered by an Eagle VIII engine and a redesigned nacelle with dual controls for an instructor and student pilot.

Vickers-Saunders BS.1 Valentia

Development

A product of specification N.3(b) for a replacement for the venerable Felixstowe F.5, the Valentia (originally, briefly known as the Valencia from 4 to 18 September 1918) was one of only a handful of government-funded projects to survive the post-war cuts and to appear during the early 1920s. Three aircraft were ordered in May 1918 – N124, N125 and N126 – as long-range twin-engined reconnaissance flying-boats.

Design

The joint venture saw the flight structures designed and built at the Vickers site at Barrow-in-Furness and the all-wooden hull built by Saunders at Cowes. The aircraft was based on the F.5s configuration, although the hull had slab sides instead of the traditional Linton-Hope sponsons. Some redesign work was carried out by Vickers at Weybridge, such as the Pierson-type biplane tail, but the majority was carried out by Saunders. One of the key features of the Valentia was a Saunders' technique called Consuta, which was very durable plywood reinforced with copper wire sown longitudinally through the ply. Consuta was ideal for skinning the hulls of flying-boats, and the Valentia was the first such machine to make full use of it.

Service

The first aircraft, N124, was launched at Cowes on 2 March 1921, for seaworthiness trials and on 5 March it was flown by Stan Cockerell from there for the first time. N124 had a troubled start, crash-landing at Newhaven during its delivery flight to Grain in April and again on 14 June, causing the prow to collapse. The aircraft was dismantled at Grain in June 1921 and remained there until at least March 1922.

N125 followed, but this too had to force-land into the sea off Bexhill on 15 March 1922, during a delivery flight to Grain. The crew on this flight was Cockerell and Capt A. Whitten-Brown of transatlantic Vimy fame. N126 first flew in March 1923 and arrived safely at Grain the following month for flight trials. A good top speed seems to have been the only positive outcome from these trials, which saw the final Valentia SOC by November 1924, having been tested with a COW gun in the nose.

Technical data – BS.1 Valentia	
ENGINES	Two 650hp Rolls-Royce Condor IAs
WINGSPAN	112ft
LENGTH	58ft
WING AREA	432 sq ft
EMPTY WEIGHT	10,000lb
ALL-UP WEIGHT	21,300 lb
MAX SPEED	105mph
ENDURANCE	4hrs 30min

The third and final Vickers-Saunders BS.1 Valentia, N126, pictured at Grain in April 1923 after delivery for type trials.

Vernon Mk I, II and III

Development
The Vernon family of aircraft was the final development of the Vimy Commercial and Vimy Ambulance. The aircraft was originally designated as a troop transport, but evolved into a bomber transport.

Design
The Vernon was a very similar aircraft to the Vimy Commercial, and the first 20, built as Mk Is, also used the same 375hp Rolls-Royce Eagle VIII engine. The Vernon had no defensive armament but could be fitted with bomb racks, the aircraft proving to be just as effective in this role as a purpose-built machine. The spacious fuselage was fully exploited by the RAF, not only to carry troops, but also heavy bulky loads. As the type was being used in the Middle East, the Eagle engines failed to deliver the power needed in very hot conditions.

The solution was obviously more power: the Mk II was fitted with a pair of 450hp Napier Lion II engines, and the Mk III with Lion III high-compression powerplants. The Mk III also had larger fuel tanks and an oleo-pneumatic undercarriage, while the nose-wheel arrangement, which was fitted to the Mk I and II, was removed.

Service
Initially flown in 1921, the first Vernons joined 45 Squadron at Almaza, Egypt, in February 1922 and 70 Squadron at Baghdad West, Iraq, in November 1922. The Vernon would be a common sight across the Middle East for the next five years, the type not only being used for troop delivery and evacuation, but also to pioneer the Cairo–Baghdad air mail service. The postal task was operated by both squadrons, which gave their aircraft personal names, Imperial Airways style, such as *Ancaeus*, *Argo*, *Aurora*, *Morpheus*, *Vagabond*, *Vaivode*, *Valkyrie*, *Venus* and *Vesuvius*. 70 Squadron retired its Vernons in December 1926, and they were replaced by the Vickers Victoria, which continued the bomber-transport role. 45 Squadron, on the other hand, converted to the DH.9A in April 1927, and became a dedicated bomber squadron right through to the 1960s.

Production
In total, 55 Vernons were built for the RAF beginning with an order for 30 Mk I aircraft under contract 121877/21 at a price of £6,000 each. These were built in the serial range J6864–J6893, although J6884–J6893 (10) were delivered as Mk IIs. Fifteen more Mk IIs were ordered under contracts 375419/22 and 424489/23 in the serial ranges J6976–J6980 and J7133–J7142, respectively. The final batch was for ten Mk IIIs, serialled J7539–J7548 under contract 511657/24 at £6,200 each.

Technical data – Vernon Mk I	
ENGINE	(Mk I) Two 375hp Rolls-Royce Eagle VIIIs; (Mk II) Two 450hp Napier Lion IIs
WINGSPAN	68ft
LENGTH	43ft 8in
HEIGHT	15ft 3in
EMPTY WEIGHT	7,890lb
GROSS WEIGHT	12,500lb
MAX SPEED	118mph
ABSOLUTE CEILING	11,700ft
RANGE	320 miles at 80mph

Originally built as a Vimy Ambulance, JR-6904 (The 'R' stands for reconditioned) was converted to a Vernon Mk III and taken on strength by 70 Squadron in June 1924. The aircraft also served with 45 Squadron and was finally used as a test-bed for a pair of Rolls-Royce Condor engines.

Vulcan (Type 61, 63 and 74)

Development

The Vickers Vulcan was an attempt to offer the struggling airline industry a relatively inexpensive aircraft with low running costs. Designed to replace or complement the Airco 18 class of aircraft, the Vulcan also took advantage of war surplus Eagle VIII engines and was offered at an appealing £2,500; a figure that could be just about managed by newly established airlines with little capital to play with.

Design

The design of the Vulcan centred on a capacious fuselage very similar to the Vimy Commercial and structurally followed similar lines to the Vimy line of aircraft. The main sections of the wings were made up of spruce box-spars, which supported a line of profile ribs, also made of spruce, all braced internally with wooden struts and tie-rods. The forward section of the fuselage was built up from wooden box-formers, which were elliptical in shape, while the rear fuselage was a trussed tie-rod braced wooden structure, which was fabric-covered.

Pierson's biplane tail structure was used again simply because the required strength was still lacking in the materials needed for a single-cantilever surface. The pilot was located in a single-seat cockpit, which was positioned, rather exposed, directly in front of the upper main plane, but this did give him an excellent view. The Vulcan's passengers were accommodated in a capacious cabin with large unobstructed windows.

Service

Instone Air Lines was the first to order three Vulcans, in December 1921, direct from the drawing board; the first of these, G-EBBL, was registered in February 1922 and undertook its maiden flight in April. Nicknamed the 'Flying Pig' by Instone staff, the aircraft entered service with the airline from 1 June 1922, on the London to Paris route. Two Vulcans were ordered by Qantas, but only one, G-EBET, was actually delivered – only to be returned because the specification set by the Australian airline could not be met.

Three Vickers Vulcan biplane transports passed through Imperial Airways' inventory between 1924 and 1928. The first of these was the ex-Instone Airways' machine, G-EBBL, originally named *City of Antwerp* but renamed *City of Brussels* when it was acquired in March 1924. The aircraft also had a short career with Imperial Airways, but the Eagle-powered machine had been withdrawn by May 1924.

Production

Eight Vulcans were built the prototype Type 61, G-EBBL (£1,800 for Instone), G-EBDH (£2,500 for Instone), G-EBEA (£2,500 for Instone), G-EBEM (ordered by the Air Ministry as a freight carrier; sold for charter work; £1,000), G-EBES (for Qantas but not completed) and G-EBET (for Qantas but returned as the specification was not met); one Type 63, G-EBEK (£3,200); and one Type 74, G-EBLB (£2,000 for Imperial Airways).

Technical data – Vulcan Type 61 & Type 74	
ENGINE	(61) One 360hp Rolls-Royce Eagle VIII and (G-EBEK) one Eagle IX; (74) One 450hp Napier Lion
WINGSPAN	49ft
LENGTH	(61) 37ft 6in; (74) 42ft 8in
HEIGHT	14ft 3in
WING AREA	840 sq ft
EMPTY WEIGHT	(61) 3,775lb; (74) 4,400lb
GROSS WEIGHT	(61) 6,150lb; (74) 6,750lb
MAX SPEED	(61) 105mph at sea level; (74) 112mph at sea level
ABSOLUTE CEILING	(61) 9,500ft; (74) 10,500ft
RANGE	(61) 360 miles; (74) 430 miles

The second of just three Type 61 Vulcans ordered by Instone Air Line Ltd was G-EBDH, which was delivered in July 1922. The aircraft had a short career and was withdrawn from use in July 1923.

Virginia Mk I to Mk X

Development

The Vickers Virginia bridged a gap in the RAF inventory from 1924 through to 1937, when it was replaced by a new era of bomber aircraft, like the Wellington, Hampden and Whitley. It was developed into a host of variants from the Mk I to the Mk X, the latter only displaying a passing resemblance to the original aircraft.

Design

The Virginia was designed to replace another Vickers stalwart, the Vimy, with work beginning in 1920. A pair of prototypes were ordered in January 1921 at a cost of £13,250 each, the first of them, J6856, flying from Brooklands on 24 November 1922.

The prototype was powered by a pair of Napier Lion engines inside rectangular nacelles mounted on the lower wing. All Virginias in RAF service had the engine position modified to be above the lower wing, housed inside a small, neat nacelle. The Mk III to the Mk V had the same wing layout as the prototype, with the lower wing having a dihedral and a straight leading edge. From the Mk VII onwards, the forward fuselage was redesigned and strengthened, and the wings were slightly swept back from the centre section. The Mk IX and Mk X had a rear gunner's position in the tail. While the Mk IX was mainly constructed from wood like its predecessors, the Mk X was all metal with a fabric covering, and the vertical tail surfaces were modified. The Mk X also introduced Handley Page slats, and the very last production aircraft were fitted with a tail wheel rather than a skid.

Service

The Virginia first joined the RAF on 6 June 1924, when Mk III J6992, fitted with dual controls, joined 7 Squadron at Bircham Newton. 58 Squadron at Worthy Down was the first unit to receive the Mk V in December 1924, while 7 Squadron received the first Mk VI in June 1925. 58 Squadron was also the first unit to take delivery of the Mk VII in January 1927, while 9 Squadron was the first to receive the Mk IX. The final variant, the Virginia Mk X, was delivered to 58 Squadron in January 1928.

The Virginia served with ten RAF squadrons; the last, 51 Squadron at Boscombe Down phased out the Mk X in favour of the Whitley in February 1938. As well as those units already mentioned, the Virginia also served with 10, 75, 214, 215, 500 and 502 squadrons.

Production

In total, 124 Virginias were built in eight different versions, beginning with a pair of Mk Is (Type 57 and 76), J6856 and J6857 in 1922. Six Mk IIIs (Type 79s) were built, J6992 and J6993 and J7129–J7132; two Mk IVs (Type 99s), J7274 and J7275; 22 Mk Vs (Type 100s), J7418–J7439; 25 Mk VIs (Type 108s), J7558 to J7567 and J7706–J7720; 11 Mk VIIs (Type 112s), J8236–J8241 and J8326–J8330; eight Mk IX (Type 128s), J8907–J8914 and 50 Mk Xs (Type 139), serialled K2321–K2339 and K2650–K2680.

Technical data – Virginia Mk I, VII & X	
ENGINE	(I) Two 450hp Napier Lions; (VII) Two 500hp Napier Lion Vs; (X) Two 580hp Napier Lion VBs
WINGSPAN	(I & VII) 86ft 6in; (X) 87ft 8in
LENGTH	(I & VII) 50ft 7in; (X) 62ft 3in
HEIGHT	(I) 17ft 3in; (VII) 16ft 11in; (X) 18ft 2in
WING AREA	(I & VII) 2,166 sq ft; (X) 2,178 sq ft
EMPTY WEIGHT	(I & VII) 9,243lb; (X) 9,650lb
GROSS WEIGHT	(I) 16,750lb; (VII) 16,500lb; (X) 17,600lb
MAX SPEED	(I) 97mph at sea level; (VII) 104mph at sea level; (X) 108mph at 5,000ft
SERVICE CEILING	(I) 8,700ft; (VII) 7,420ft; (X) 15,530ft
RANGE	(I) 1,000 miles at 75mph; (VII) 980 miles at 100mph and 5,000ft; (X) 985 miles at 100mph and 5,000ft

Right: Virginia Mk X 'K' of 7 Squadron at Worthy Down running up its Napier Lion VB engines prior to embarking on a night training sortie. The unit operated the Virginia from May 1924 to March 1936.

Below: One of 25 Mk VIs built was J7715, another busy aircraft that served the RAF and Vickers from September 1925 to September 1936.

Victoria Mk I to VI and Valentia

Development

Intended as a replacement for the Vernon, the Victoria had the same lineage with the Virginia bomber as the Vernon had with the Vimy.

Design

Designed to Air Ministry specification 5/20, which called for a troop carrier biplane, the Victoria comfortably won the contract, with the only competition being the Bristol Type 56. Two prototypes were ordered, the aircraft becoming the Mk I and Mk II; production aircraft being designated from the Mk III onwards. The two early aircraft only differed from the later machines by having a dihedral on the lower wing, and, like the Virginia prototype before it, the engines, Napier Lion IAX in this case, were mounted directly onto the wings rather than raised above it.

The first production version, the Mk III, was fitted with sweptback wings and metal structures rather than the all-wood of the prototypes. Several Mk IIIs were converted to Mk IV standard with metal outer wings and Handley Page slats. The Mk V was the first all-metal Victoria with Lion XIB engines, and featured all-moving fins and rudders. The final version, the Mk VI, was fitted with Pegasus engines and a tail wheel rather than a skid. The Valentia was a re-engined version of the Victoria Mk IV, and as well as 28 new-builds, 54 were converted from Victorias with Pegasus II L3 or M3 radials.

Service

First flown in January 1926, the Victoria Mk III entered service proper with 70 Squadron at Hinaidi in February, although a Mk I had been attached to the unit since January 1924. The second Middle Eastern unit to receive the Victoria, 216 Squadron at Heliopolis, followed in July 1924. The type was also allocated to the Bomber Transport Flight in India while the Valentia, as well as 70 and 216 squadrons, also served with 31 Squadron from Lahore between April 1939 and August 1941, marking the end of the Vickers biplane transports in service.

Production

In total, 97 Victorias were built; all were delivered to the RAF between 1926 and 1933. Two prototypes (Type 56 (Mk I) and 81 (Mk II)) priced at £13,690 each, J6860 and J6861, were delivered in October 1922 and February 1923, respectively. Fourty-six Mk IIIs, J7921–J7935, J8061–J8066, J8226–J8235 and J8915–J8929 (13 were later converted to Mk IV). One Mk IV prototype (Type 145), J9250, was built; 37 Mk Vs, J9760–J9766, K1310–K1315, K2340–K2345 and K2791–K2808 (11 were later converted to Mk IVs; and a further 28 were converted to Valentia standard [54 Victorias were converted to Valentias]). Eleven Mk IVs (Type 262s), K3159–K3169, were delivered between September and December 1933.

Technical data – Victoria Mk I, V, VI & Valentia	
ENGINE	(I) Two 450hp Napier Lion IAXs; (III) Two 450hp Napier Lion IIs; (V) Two 570hp Napier Lion XIBs; (VI) Two 660hp Bristol Pegasus IIL3s; (Valentia) Two 635hp Bristol Pegasus IIM3s
WINGSPAN	(I) 86ft 6in; (V, VI & Valentia) 87ft 4in
LENGTH	(I) 51ft 7in; (V, VI & Valentia) 59ft 6in
HEIGHT	(I) 17ft 3in; (V, VI & Valentia) 17ft 9in
WING AREA	(V, VI & Valentia) 2,178 sq ft
EMPTY WEIGHT	(I) 10,155lb; (V) 10,030lb; (VI) 9,806lb; (Valentia) 10,994lb
GROSS WEIGHT	(I) 18,100lb; (V) 17,760lb; (VI) 17,600lb; (Valentia) 19,500lb
MAX SPEED	(I) 106mph at sea level; (V) 110mph at sea level; (VI) 130mph at 5,000ft; (Valentia) 120mph at 5,000ft
SERVICE CEILING	(V) 16,200ft; (Valentia) 16,250ft
RANGE	(I); 400 miles; (V) 770 miles; (VI & Valentia) 800 miles

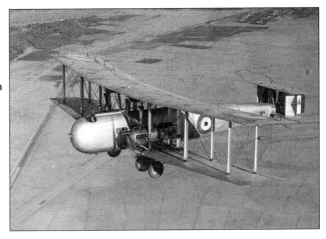

Right: One of the first Victoria Mk IIIs to enter RAF service was J7924, which joined 70 Squadron in 1926. The aircraft is over Hinaidi, where the unit operated from between 1922 and 1937.

Below left: The fact there is not a pilot visible in the cockpit, and this is clearly not a model, gives away that this Victoria Mk V, K2344, is conducting blind flying tests while with the Central Flying School.

Below right: The Victoria was designed to carry 22 fully armed troops over a range of approximately 800 miles.

Vixen Mk I to IV, Vivid and Valiant

Development

Building on the experience gained from the F.B.14, Vickers decided to attempt to expand its sales by designing a general-purpose fighter/reconnaissance/bomber aircraft. Conferences were held with the Air Ministry before the private venture was embarked upon, which gave Rex Pierson the opportunity to design a machine to replace the F.2b fighter or the D.H.9a.

Design

The Vixen was a single-bay biplane powered by the reliable 450hp Napier Lion; an engine that had not been available to the wartime F.B.14. Construction comprised a steel tube for the fuselage and wood for the wings, and the first aircraft, designated as the Vixen I (Type 71), G-EBEC, initially flew from Brooklands in February 1923. Flight tests at Martlesham Heath were encouraging, and, once returned to Vickers, the aircraft was modified into the Vixen II (Type 87). Changes included a new ventral radiator positioned between the undercarriage struts. The Vixen II was first flown on 23 August 1923, the aircraft later being used as a testbed for a new Vickers machine gun to replace the Lewis. Once again, reports from Martlesham were good, and as a result a contract for six aircraft, to specification 45/23, was signed.

The Vixen III (Type 91) was a new aircraft, registered as G-EBIP, which completed its maiden flight from Brooklands in April 1924. The Mk III had much larger wings, which improved performance at altitude and its radiator was repositioned back into the nose. After flight testing in land and water configurations, G-EBIP went on to compete in three King's Cup races from 1925 to 1927; the best result was in the last race, when the machine came second. It was the Mk III that led to the most successful Vixen, the Mk V (Type 116), which was powered by a Napier Lion Mk V high-compression engine with a modified tail unit; 18 of this mark were ordered by Chile.

G-EBEC was converted again to become the Vixen Mk IV (Type 105) night-fighter, powered by a Rolls-Royce Condor engine. Performance was only marginally improved, so the aircraft was converted again to become the Vixen Mk VI (Type 124). This time, the larger wings of the Mk III were fitted, and the aircraft was entered as a general-purpose aircraft for specification 26/27.

As a result of the problems with the Chilean Vixen Mk V's wings, Vickers produced a version with metal wings, which was, at first, called the Vixen VII, but was quickly renamed the Vivid (Type 130). First flown on 27 June 1927, the aircraft was initially powered by a Napier Lion VA, but after being fitted with a Napier Lion XI, the designation changed again, and it became the Type 146.

Service

The Chilean Air Force ordered a dozen Vixen Mk Vs in May 1925, which was increased to 18 aircraft by July of that year. Operated by the Grupo Mixto Aviación No. 3, the Vixen served into the 1930s and, by all accounts, was a popular aircraft with air and ground crew alike.

Production

Vixen: Twenty aircraft were built, beginning with Mk I, II, IV and VI (Type 71, 87, 105 and 126) G-EBEC; Mk III (Type 91 and 148) G-EBIP; and 18 Mk Vs (Type 116) for Chile serialled V1–V18.

Vivid: One aircraft, G-EBPY (Type 130), ex-G-EBIP, was sold to J. R. Chaplin for £300 on 31 March 1931.
Valiant: One aircraft, GEBVM (Type 131), was used as a private-venture demonstrator for Chile.

Technical data – Vixen Mk I, V, Vivid & Valiant	
ENGINE	(I) One 450hp Napier Lion I; (V) one 500hp Napier Lion V; (Vivid) One Napier Lion VA or XI; (Valiant) One 455hp Bristol Jupiter VI
WINGSPAN	(I upper) 40ft; (V upper) 44ft; (Valiant) 45ft 7in
LENGTH	29ft; (Valiant) 34ft
HEIGHT	(I) 13ft; (V) 12ft
WING AREA	(I) 526 sq ft; (V & Valiant) 590 sq ft
EMPTY WEIGHT	(I) 3,098lb; (V) 3,320lb; (Valiant) 2,973lb
GROSS WEIGHT	(I) 4,720lb; (V) 5,080lb; (Valiant) 5,550lb
MAX SPEED	(I) 137mph at 10,000ft; (V) 133.7mph at ground level; (Valiant) 125mph at ground level
CEILING	(I service) 19,400ft; (V absolute) 20,000ft; (Valiant) 21,800ft
RANGE	(V) 764 miles

Above left: Vixen Mk III G-EBIP during float-plane trials at the Marine Aircraft Experimental Establishment (MAEE), Felixstowe, on 26 January 1927.

Above right: G-EBEC, in its original guise as the Vixen Mk I (Type 71), complete with short fuselage and a car-type radiator mounted on the front.

The sole Vivid, G-EBPY, was sold to J. R. Chaplin in March 1931 for just £300. Along with Capt T. Neville Stack, the duo set a host of out-and-back records with the aircraft, including flights from the UK to Berlin, Copenhagen and Warsaw. The pair pose for the camera prior to flying to Australia and back, which they achieved in 28 days.

Vanguard

Development
The Vickers Type 62 Vanguard was a twin-engined biplane, capable of carrying 23 passengers. The aircraft came about because of an enquiry from Instone Air Lines for a single aircraft.

Design
The aircraft was similar in appearance to the Victoria, but was actually based upon the Virginia Mk I. The fuselage was an all-wood monocoque, very similar to the Victoria, but it was widened to provide a higher standard of comfort for civilian passengers.

The lower centre section, outer and upper main planes, installation of the two Napier Lion engines and the undercarriage were exactly the same as those used on the Virginia and Victoria. The upper main section was made wider to ensure the new broader fuselage would fit into place, but the tail unit remained the same as that used on the Virginia and Victoria.

As the design was progressing, the Air Ministry began to show an interest, inviting Vickers to tender to specification 1/22, which called for a 23-seat commercial aircraft. Once the proposal was submitted, the Air Ministry ordered one aircraft, to be named Vanguard and given the registration G-EBCP and the military serial J6924.

Service
The Vanguard completed its maiden flight from Brooklands on 18 July 1923, in the hands of Stan Cockerell. After a small amount of tweaking, the Vanguard quickly established a reputation as a lovely aircraft to fly; this was endorsed by many service pilots who flew it during trials at Martlesham Heath.

It was obvious at an early stage that the Vanguard could handle more power, and after being re-engined with a pair of 650hp Condor III engines, it was redesignated as the Type 103. The Condor engines improved the Vanguard even further, but it may have been a sign of the gathering economic problems that G-EBCP was destined to remain the only aircraft, despite interest from around the globe.

G-EBCP was reconditioned and redesignated as the Type 170 before it was loaned to Imperial Airways in May 1928, and it was then immediately employed on the London–Paris service and later the London–Brussels–Cologne route. In October 1928, the aircraft was returned to Vickers only to be lost during a flight test on 16 May 1929, when the aircraft crashed at Shepperton. Sadly, the accident claimed the lives of Vickers test pilot Edward 'Tiny' Scholefield and his flight observer Frank Sherratt. The cause was never fully established, but it is believed that all-flying rudders had been fitted by Vickers, similar to those fitted on the Virginia Mk X. As a result, Scholefield may have over stressed the rudders and lost control.

Technical data – Vanguard	
ENGINE	Two 468hp Napier Lions; Two 650hp Rolls-Royce Condor IIIs
WINGSPAN	87ft 9in
LENGTH	53ft 10in
WING AREA	2,182 sq ft
EMPTY WEIGHT	12,040lb
GROSS WEIGHT	18,500lb
MAX SPEED	112mph
CEILING	16,400ft
CLIMB RATE	476 ft/min

Built as the Type 62 with Napier Lion engines, the Vanguard became the Type 103, with Condor powerplant (shown here), and, as the Type 170, it served briefly with Imperial Airways.

Viget

Development

Organised by the Royal Aero Club in 1923, the Lympne Light Aeroplane Trials were an attempt to promote cheap opportunities to operate private aircraft. Each aircraft, which was actually designated as a 'motor glider', was to be a single seater with power provided by an engine no greater than 750cc. A host of prizes were up for grabs for categories such as the lowest fuel consumption and greatest aggregate mileage. The event had several sponsors, including the Duke of Sutherland and the Daily Mail, which put up £1,500.

Design

Designed by Rex Pierson, the Type 92 Viget was a single-bay biplane with unstaggered, constant chord wings, which could be folded as per one of the many rules of the competition. Only the lower wing had a slight dihedral and full-span ailerons were fitted to both main planes.

The fuselage was deeper than it was wide, and the single-axle undercarriage was attached to the front and rear wing spars. Power was provided by a 750cc Douglas motorcycle engine, which was mounted horizontally with its cylinder heads poking out of the lower cowling.

Service

The Viget, registered as G-EBHN, was first flown by Stan Cockerell just prior to the Lympne trials and was said to handle very well for such a small, under-powered machine. Cockerell flew the Viget during the trials, but failed to win any of the individual competitions. The aircraft's competition ended when a rocker arm broke, and, without causing any damage to the aircraft, Cockerell force-landed in a field near Brabourne, approximately six miles from Lympne. Rather than leave the little aircraft, Cockerell folded the wings and proceeded to walk the aircraft back to Lympne.

Part way along his journey, Cockerell dropped into a pub for some liquid refreshment, only to find a large group of people sitting and standing around the Viget when he came out. To his amusement, he was asked by several of them when the next performance was going to begin! The crowd had mistaken the folded Viget as a travelling Punch and Judy show!

Advertising the aircraft in 1924 as appropriate for 'Sports, commercial and training purposes', Vickers tried and failed to market the Viget, even offering it with a Bristol Cherub or Blackburne-type engine.

Technical data – Viget	
ENGINE	One 750cc Douglas
WINGSPAN	25ft
LENGTH	17ft 4in
WING AREA	200 sq ft
EMPTY WEIGHT	390lb
LOADED WEIGHT	570lb
MAX SPEED	58.1mph

Vickers "Viget" Single-Seater Light Aeroplane.

A smiling Stan Cockerell sits in the cockpit of the diminutive Type 89 Viget, which was entered into the 1923 Lympne Light (Aeroplane) Trials.

Venture

Development

Specification 45/23 was a fiercely contested competition for a new general-purpose two-seat armed reconnaissance aircraft to replace the D.H.9A, which saw Vickers enter three different aircraft, the Valiant, the Vixen and the Venture. Five other aircraft were also submitted, of which one of them, the Westland Wapiti, would be the ultimate winner.

An order for six aircraft was placed by the Air Ministry, but initially Vickers had trouble offering the new machine with an appropriate name beginning with 'V'. The ministry was initially offered the name Vulpes (the common fox) and Vortex, but eventually Venture was settled upon.

Design

The Venture was a combination of Vickers components; for example, the controls, wooden main planes and propeller were from the Vixen Mk II, while the extended-type steel tube fuselage, low-positioned radiator, tail and chassis came from the Vixen Mk III.

Service

The first Venture, J7277, undertook its maiden flight from Brooklands on 3 June 1924, and on 17 June was delivered to the A&AEE at Martlesham Heath. The aircraft was well received by service test pilots, recording a maximum speed of 135mph with a full military load and good general handling. The remaining five aircraft were all completed in the same week: J7279 was delivered on 4 July; J7278 the following day; and J7280, J7281 and J7282 all on 9 July.

Despite the early favourable reports coming out of Martlesham, in September 1924 the Air Ministry declared that the aircraft would be unsuitable. Among the reasons given were that the Venture was too large, the pilot had a poor downward view, longitudinal stability was inadequate, and the aircraft's landing run was too long. Vickers made several attempts to improve these points, but no more were ordered, and all six aircraft were dispersed to various military units. These included some service trials with 2 Squadron, the RAE and further time with the A&AEE. J7277 remained on RAF charge until January 1933.

Production

Six Venture Mk Is (Type 94), serialled J7277–J7282, were ordered under contract 483332/24, dated March 1924, to specification 45/23 at £2,700 each.

Technical data – Venture	
ENGINE	One 450hp Napier Lion I
WINGSPAN	40ft
LENGTH	32ft
WING AREA	526 sq ft
EMPTY WEIGHT	3,140lb
LOADED WEIGHT	4,890lb
MAX SPEED	129mph at 10,000ft

Vixen Mk III G-EBIP during float-plane trials at MAEE, Felixstowe, on 26 January 1927.

Vagabond

Development

Following on from the success of the 1923 Lympne Light Aeroplane Trials, the Royal Aero Club continued the event the following year, but this time changed the criteria to a two-seat aircraft powered by a 1,100cc engine and, once again, fitted with folding wings for ease of storage and transportation.

Design

Again designed by Rex Pierson, Vickers' entrant in the 1924 competition was the Type 98 Vagabond, a single-bay biplane with constant chord staggered wings. Full length ailerons were fitted to both main planes and flaps to the inner lower, which could be folded so as not to interfere with the main plane fold. The pilot had good visibility, aided by a cut-out in the centre rear of the upper main plane.

The fuselage was rounder than the Viget, and power was provided by a flat twin 32hp Bristol Cherub III engine, which was mounted within an aerodynamic nose. The fin and rudder were also more rounded than the Viget, while the horizontal stabiliser was virtually identical. Mounted forward of the lower wing because of the amount of stagger, the undercarriage was fixed to the lower fuselage longeron at the front, and to the front wing spar at the rear.

Tail trimming was carried out in one of the most novel ways ever designed into an aircraft. Instead of the traditional method of changing the angle of the tailplane, the entire rear fuselage of the Vagabond was hinged behind the rear cockpit. A handwheel mounted between the two cockpits was turned to either increase drag on landing or lessen it during take-off and normal flight.

Service

The sole Vagabond was registered as G-EBJF on 1 July 1924, and early flight trials were carried out by Pierson's technical assistant H. J. Payn, who would occasionally act as a Vickers' test pilot. Before the aircraft was entered for the trials, the Cherub was replaced by a 1,095cc Blackburne Thrush radial engine, but unfortunately it only took part in the preliminary rounds before the aircraft was eliminated from the competition.

It is not known if the Vagabond was marketed in the same way as the Viget; either way the aircraft was neither successful during the Lympne trials nor as a commercial venture and was deregistered on 24 January 1928.

Technical data – Vagabond	
ENGINE	One 32hp Bristol Cherub; One 1,095cc Blackburne Thrush
WINGSPAN	28ft
LENGTH	21ft 10in
WING AREA	235 sq ft
EMPTY WEIGHT	527lb
LOADED WEIGHT	887lb
MAX SPEED	77mph

Type 91 Vagabond G-EBJF, with the Bristol Cherub engine in place, before it briefly took part in 1924 Lympne trials.

Valparaiso I, II and III and Valiant

Development

As interest began to grow in the Vixen family of aircraft, orders were being accepted by Vickers from overseas customers. In order to distinguish these aircraft from potential home orders, the name of the aircraft was changed from Vixen to Valparaiso (the name of a Chilean city, even though the majority of the orders were from Portugal).

Design

In November 1923, an order was placed by Portugal for four Rolls-Royce Eagle-powered Vixen Mk Is and ten more powered by Napier lion engines. These were renamed Valparaisos, the Lion-powered aircraft being designated as the Mk I, and the Eagle-powered, the Mk II. The first aircraft of the order was originally just called the Vickers Type V, but was later sold to Chile as a Valparaiso Mk I. The aircraft made its maiden flight on 24 August 1924, and after flight testing was found to perform the same as the Vixen Mk I, G-EBEC.

A licence-built version of the Valparaiso, powered with a Gnome-Rhône Jupiter VIa air-cooled radial engine, was designated as the Mk III. The conversion work was carried out at Weybridge, and the first aircraft flew from there on 28 July 1929. Coupled with the French-built powerplant, 13 Valparaisos were built by General Aeronautical Material Workshops (OGMA) in Alverca, Portugal.

Service

Only one Valparaiso was supplied to Chile, but this aircraft made quite an impact when, in 1924, it raised the South American altitude record to 20,000ft. This one event alone contributed greatly towards a subsequent order for Vixen Mk Vs for the Chilean Air Force.

In Portuguese service, the Valparaisos were popular aircraft with their crews as well as the general public, who were often treated to breathtaking flying at air displays. Records were also broken, the most significant taking place in May 1928, when two Valparaiso Mk Is flew to the Portuguese colonies in Africa, Angola and Mozambique and back in 94 flying hours, covering a distance of 11,500 miles.

The Valparaiso gave the Portuguese Air Force good and long service, 20 years of which were with the Grupo de Esquadrilhas de Aviacao Republica in 1934 and four made a goodwill tour of Northern France in 1935. By the following year, though, the type had been withdrawn.

Production

Ten Valparaiso Mk Is (Type 93s) and four Mk IIs (Type 92s) were built for Portugal at a cost of £5,070 each and delivered on 29 July 1924. A single Mk I (Type 102) was supplied to Chile and one Mk III (Type 108) prototype was modified by Vickers to take a Gnome-Rhône Jupiter engine. A further 13 were licence-built by OGMA in Portugal and serialled 200–212.

The only Valiant built, which was based on the Vivid, was also supplied to Chile in 1928, but was wrecked in an accident in March 1929.

Technical data – Valparaiso I & Valiant	
ENGINE	(Valparaiso Mk I) One 468hp Napier Lion IA; (Valiant) One 455hp Bristol Jupiter VI
WINGSPAN	(Valparaiso upper) 40ft; (Valiant) 45ft 7in
LENGTH	(Valparaiso) 29ft; (Valiant) 34ft
HEIGHT	(Valparaiso) 11ft 8in; (Valiant) 13ft
WING AREA	(Valparaiso) 526 sq ft; (Valiant) 590 sq ft
EMPTY WEIGHT	(Valparaiso) 3,128lb; (Valiant) 2,973lb
GROSS WEIGHT	(Valparaiso) 4,720lb; (Valiant) 5,550lb
MAX SPEED	(Valparaiso) 136mph at 10,000ft; (Valiant) 125mph at ground level
CEILING	(Valparaiso service) 19,500ft; (Valiant absolute) 21,800ft
RANGE	(Valparaiso) 550 miles at 110mph at 10,000ft

Capts Ramos and Viegas pose in front of one of the Valparaiso Mk Is, in which they flew to the Portuguese colonies and back in May 1928. The record-breaking flight took 94 flying hours and covered a distance of 11,500 miles.

Vespa Mk I to VI

Development

Built as a private venture in response to military specification 30/24 for a two-seat reconnaissance and army co-operation aircraft, the Vickers Vespa competed against the de Havilland Hyena and Short Chamois as a replacement for the long-serving F.2B; however, none of them would prove better than the machine designed to fight during World War One.

Design

The Vespa was a tractor biplane, powered by a Bristol Jupiter IV engine mounted on the front of a slim-fuselage, between lightly loaded and staggered twin-bay wings. First flown in September 1925, Vespa Mk I G-EBLD was delivered to Martlesham Heath in February 1926 but failed to secure an order from the RAF on the back of 30/24. After an engine failure in June 1926, the aircraft was rebuilt with a Jupiter VI engine, metal wings and various other modifications following the earlier trial. Redesignated as the Vespa Mk II, the aircraft was once again delivered for service trials, the machine's STOL capability and improved maximum altitude to 21,700ft doing nothing to convince the RAF to order.

However, by this time, the Vespa had attracted interest from Bolivia, and an all-metal version was produced, specifically for the South American country as the Mk III. An Mk IV version, powered by an Armstrong Siddeley Jaguar VIC, was built for the Irish Air Corps (IAC) and the Mk V, also for the IAC, was modified with a townend ring.

The Vespa Mk VI was G-ABIL rebuilt as a demonstrator for the Chinese Central Government, while the final variant was the Mk VII, which was powered by a Pegasus 'S' engine and flown by Cyril Uwins on 16 September 1932, to capture the World Height Record at 43,976ft.

Service

The Vespa first entered military service with the Bolivian Air Force in 1928, when six Mk IIIs were delivered. The aircraft were generally used as training and conversion aircraft, but at least two saw action during the Chaco War (1932–1935) between Bolivia and Paraguay. A Vespa Flight was also believed to have been operated, made up of a single fully armed Vespa, which could go into action at a moment's notice with a pair of Vickers Type 143 Scouts as escort.

The IAC operated four Mk IVs and four Mk Vs from Baldonnel throughout the 1930s until 12 June 1940, when the last aircraft was written off in an accident.

Production

One Mk I (Type 113), G-EBLD, was built to specification 30/24, which was later converted to an Mk II (Type 119). Six Mk IIIs (Type 149s) were built for Bolivia; four Mk IVs (Type 193s) for Irish Air Corps (IAC) and four Mk Vs (Type 208s) also for the IAC. One Mk VI (Type 210), G-ABIL, was converted from G-ELBD for the world height record attempt, and one Mk VII (Type 250), G-ABIL, was converted and delivered to the RAE as K3588.

Technical data – Vespa Mk I, II, V & VI	
ENGINE	(I) One Bristol Jupiter IV; (II) One 455hp Jupiter VI; (V) One 490hp Armstrong Siddeley Jaguar VIC; (VI) One 530hp Bristol Jupiter VIIF
WINGSPAN	50ft
LENGTH	(II) 31ft 3in; (V) 33ft; (VI) 32ft 6in
HEIGHT	(II) 10ft 3in; (V & VI) 10ft 6in
WING AREA	(II) 561 sq ft; (V & VI) 576 sq ft
EMPTY WEIGHT	(II) 2,468lb; (V) 2,882lb; (VI) 2,917lb
GROSS WEIGHT	(II) 3,925lb; (V & VI) 4,370lb
MAX SPEED	**(II)** 129mph at 10,000ft; (V) 139mph at 10,000ft; (VI) 148.5mph at 10,000ft
SERVICE CEILING	(II) 21,700ft; (VI) 26,700ft
RANGE	(V) 580 miles at 116mph and 15,000ft

After much modification, the original Vespa Mk I, G-EBLD, was rebuilt as the final variant, the Mk VII, and re-registered as G-ABIL '0-5'. The aircraft set the World Height Record at 43,976ft on 16 September 1932.

Vendace I, II and III

Development
Issued in October 1924, specification 5A/24 called for a new floatplane trainer, which not only saw Vickers enter its Type 120 Vendace (the name of any freshwater white fish) Mk I, but also two other manufacturers with the Parnall Perch and the Blackburn Sprat.

Design
The Vendace was a tractor biplane, which, as per the specification, had folding wooden wings and a fuselage constructed of steel tubes. The aircraft could be converted from a landplane to a floatplane in just ten minutes, thanks to a Vickers oleo-pneumatic system. The machine's two cockpits were positioned close together so that instructor and student could communicate. The Vendace was powered by a 275hp Rolls-Royce Falcon III engine, which was gravity-fed by fuel from a pair of streamlined fuel tanks mounted in the central upper-section of the wing. The Air Ministry accepted the Vickers proposal, and a single aircraft was ordered in August 1925.

The sole Vendace Mk II was a private venture powered by a 300hp ADC Nimbus, while the Mk III was powered by a 300hp Hispano-Suiza 8F engine, three of which were ordered by Bolivia.

Service
Serialled N208, the Vendace Mk I first flew as a landplane from Brooklands in March 1926, and by the following month had been delivered to Coastal Area HQ at Gosport. Here, the aircraft was fitted with an arrester hook and then promptly flown to HMS *Furious* for type and deck landing trials.

The trials went well, and, by the end of the year, the landplane trials were completed and the aircraft was sent to Felixstowe on 25 March 1927 for floatplane trials. Once again, the aircraft performed well, other than some corrosion issues, but no production order was forthcoming, and the N208 remained at Felixstowe until at least February 1928.

The Vendace Mk I, which was registered as G-EBPX on 3 January 1927, was first flown in November of that year. The aircraft was only used as a demonstrator, but after a successful presentation in April 1928, the aircraft was bought by the Aircraft Operating Company (AOC) for £2,750 in June and was employed on aerial survey work across South America.

In October 1928, Bolivia placed an order for three aircraft, designated as the Vendace Mk III, with the intention of operating them as trainers. Many Bolivian pilots are believed to have begun their flying training on the Vendace before converting to the Vespa or Bolivian Scout.

Production
One Vendace Mk I (Type 120), N208, was ordered under contract 615049/25 at a cost of £3,225; one Mk II (Type 133), G-EBPX, was built as a private venture demonstrator and three Mk IIIs (Type 155s) built for Bolivia were delivered on 1 October 1928. G-EBPX was converted to Type 157 and sold to the AOC on 1 June 1928.

Technical data – Vendace I (Land & Sea) & III	
ENGINE	(I) One 270hp Rolls-Royce Falcon III; (III) One 300hp Hispano-Suiza 8F
WINGSPAN	44ft 7in
LENGTH	(I Land) 32ft 3in; (I Sea) 35ft 2in; (III) 33ft 3in
HEIGHT	(I Land) 12ft 8in; (I Sea) 13ft 11½in; (III) 12ft 9in
WING AREA	(I Land & III) 533 sq ft; (I Sea) 525 sq ft
EMPTY WEIGHT	(I Land) 2,585lb; (I Sea) 2,960lb; (III) 2,604lb
GROSS WEIGHT	(I Land) 3,475lb; (I Sea) 3,850lb; (III) 3,270lb
MAX SPEED	(I Land) 117mph; (I Sea) 111mph; (III) 119mph at 13,000ft
CEILING	(I Land) 20,000ft; (I Sea) 9,470ft; (III) 25,800ft

Vickers Type 120 Vendace Mk I N208 in landplane configuration at Brooklands prior to being delivered to the Aeroplane and Armament Experimental Establishment at Martlesham Heath in August 1926.

Wibault Type 121 and 122 Scout

Development

Following Vickers' partnership with Société des Avions Michel Wibault, a single 7.C1 high-wing parasol monoplane demonstrator was ordered with a British-built Jupiter engine. Wibault, who had been working with Vickers since 1922 as a consulting engineer, was one of the pioneers of the use of metal construction, and the Wibault 7.C1 took full advantage of this.

Design

In February 1926, the 7.C1, registered in France as F-AHFH, was flown from Villacoublay to Weybridge via Croydon; the pilot, by the name of Doucy, had a tough time with the Jupiter engine because the controls had been incorrectly installed. The aircraft also featured a Vickers' oleo-pneumatic undercarriage and British flying equipment and instruments. It was also later modified with stronger wing struts so as to conform to Certificate of Airworthiness (CofA) guidelines.

The 7.C1 had an impressive top speed of 134mph and an excellent ceiling of 32,000ft; no doubt both these figures, combined with the aircrafts metal durability, helped to secure a healthy order just a few months later.

A single French-built Wibault 12.C2, which was slightly larger than the 7.C1 but had the same overall configuration, was bought by Vickers and converted to take a Lion XI engine for an Air Ministry contract.

Service

The first Wibault Scout, built by Vickers, undertook its maiden flight in June 1926. Test pilot Tiny Scholefield wisely took his parachute with him, as control was lost after several spins, forcing him to bale out at just over 1,500ft above the ground. The aircraft came down in the middle of the Vickers' sports ground at Byfleet, much to the entertainment of an elderly eyewitness who asked when the next 'exciting exhibition' of flying was going to be held! The cause was found to be a combination of a critical centre of gravity in inverted flight and the tailplane incidence being set to high.

The accident did not put off the Chileans, however, who ordered 26 Wibault Scouts, the first of them arriving in September 1926 to part-equip the Group Mixto de Aviación 1. Several were lost in accidents during their service, one losing a wing which was attributed to poor maintenance. Regardless, the Chileans were happy with the little Scout and the type remained in service until 1934.

Production

In total, 26 Vickers-Wibault Scouts (Type 121) were built under licence for Chile at a price of £3,700 each, with delivery taking place between 16 September and 27 November 1926 to El Bosque, Santiago. A single French-built Wibault 12.C2 (Type 122) serialled as J9029 was bought by Vickers to Air Ministry contract 786338/37 at a cost of £4,750.

Technical data – Wibault Type 121 & 122 Scout	
ENGINE	(121) One 455hp Bristol Jupiter VI; (122) One 500hp Hispano-Suiza
WINGSPAN	36ft 1in
LENGTH	23ft 8in
HEIGHT	11ft 6in
WING AREA	237 sq ft
EMPTY WEIGHT	1,920lb
GROSS WEIGHT	2,970lb
MAX SPEED	144mph at 15,700ft
SERVICE CEILING	23,000ft
RANGE	300 miles

The original French-built Wibault 7.C1 after its delivery from Villacoublay to Weybridge in February 1926.

Hispano, Type 141 and Bolivian Scouts

Development

It was as late as 1925 when it suddenly dawned on the Vickers' design teams that there had not been a British fighter with a liquid-cooled engine in service since the SE.5A. Rolls-Royce was developing a new liquid-cooled engine at the time, so it seemed right that Vickers, which built more SE.5As than any other aircraft manufacturer, should start to design a suitable fighter to accommodate it.

Design

Before a suitable Rolls-Royce unit was made available, Vickers purchased a 400hp Hispano-Suiza T52 for £1,200 via the Vickers-Wibault agency. The Type 123, as it would be known as no name was officially applied, was designed around this engine. The aircraft was of all-metal construction, with fabric covering the entire airframe. It was made up of duralumin sections, and the Type 123 also had a unique duralumin propeller, which had detachable blades.

First flown on 9 November 1926, the aircraft, now called the 'Hispano Scout' and registered as G-EBNQ, had reasonably good performance compared to the Wibault Scout. It was modified the following year, when a Rolls-Royce engine finally became available in the shape of a 480hp F.XI, which resulted in the aircraft being redesignated as the Type 141 Scout. In January 1928, the Type 141 was entered in an Air Ministry single-seat fighter competition at Martlesham Heath, but it failed to secure any orders, despite a good top speed. The aircraft was modified again in 1929 in response to specification 21/26 for a new fleet fighter. Unfortunately, during trials aboard HMS *Furious*, the aircraft was not tested to its full potential, and no orders were received.

However, an improved version of the Type 141, the Type 143, did gain some interest and the Bristol Jupiter-powered Bolivian Scout secured six orders from the South America country.

Service

Deliveries of the six Type 143s began in September 1929, the Bolivian Scouts becoming the first single-seat fighters to serve that country. Bolivia would have bought many more Type 143s if it had had the necessary funds, but this small band of just six fighters played an important role in familiarising the Bolivia Air Force in the art of aerial fighting.

The sixth Bolivian aircraft was fitted with a Bristol Jupiter VII engine for comparison trials with the A&AEE at Martlesham Heath. Once the Air Ministry had finished the trial, the aircraft was returned to Weybridge, re-engined with a Jupiter VIA and delivered to Bolivia.

Production

For the Type 123 Hispano Scout, one aircraft, G-EBNQ, was built as a private venture in 1926. One Type 141 Scout, G-EBNQ, was modified to specification N.21/26, and six Type 143 Bolivian Scouts were delivered between 3 September and 17 December 1929.

Technical data – Type 123 Hispano Scout & Type 143 Bolivian Scout	
ENGINE	(123) One 400hp Hispano Suiza T52; (141) One Rolls-Royce FXI; (143) One 450hp Bristol Jupiter VIA
WINGSPAN	34ft
LENGTH	(123) 28ft 6in; (143) 27ft 10½in
HEIGHT	(123) 9ft 4in; (143) 11ft 3in
WING AREA	(123) 378 sq ft; (143) 336 sq ft
EMPTY WEIGHT	(123) 2,278lb; (143) 2,246lb
LOADED WEIGHT	(123) 3,300lb; (143) 3,120lb
MAX SPEED	(123)149mph; (143) 150mph at 11,500ft
CLIMB RATE	(123) 1,515 ft/min
CEILING	(143) 20,000ft

G-EBNQ in its original form as the Type 123 Hispano Scout, which was first flown from Brooklands, on 9 November 1926.

Vireo

Development

The Vickers Type 125 Vireo was one of two aircraft that were tendered for the precise specification 17/25, which called for a Naval single-seat fighter of 'all-metal stressed-skin' construction, plus the ability to operate as a land or floatplane, and to be powered by a Lynx engine. The other entrant was the Avro Avocet, which, like the Vireo, would serve a dual-purpose from the Air Ministry's point of view: to test aircraft of all-metal construction and examine if it was feasible, or even worthwhile, operating low-powered fighters from aircraft carriers.

Design

The Vireo was constructed using the Vickers-Wibault system and structurally, with the main exception of the aircraft having a low, rather than parasol wing, it was very similar to the Chilean Wibault Scout. The aircraft could be operated with standard wheeled undercarriage or on a float chassis; both versions having the ability to be launched by catapult.

Armament was a pair of wing-mounted machine guns, which fired outside of the propeller's arc. Because of a deep wing section, a Vickers Auto RC Type (later known as the E Type) machine gun was placed in the wing, a novel feature for the day. Each weapon had an under-mounted revolver type cartridge chamber, which was controlled remotely via a linkage system. The method of firing the machine guns was an early attempt to overcome the limitations of synchronising equipment, which enabled the weapon to fire through the propeller. Earlier efforts had also been hampered because the early RAF-type air foils were just too thin to bury a machine gun in them.

Service

The Vireo first took to the air in March 1928, two and half years after the specification was issued and during which time the RAE had carried out a host of trials and tests on metal structures. The Lynx IV engine delivered less power than Vickers had hoped for, and before an improved version was delivered, the Vireo, now serialled N211, was delivered to Martlesham Heath on 30 March.

The aircraft suffered from several mechanical failures during the trial, although the most alarming trait occurred just before landing, when the aircraft had a tendency to drop a wing and stall onto the ground. Some structural damage was caused by these landings, and once repaired the aircraft was delivered to Gosport for deck landing trials aboard HMS *Furious* in July. Seaplane trials were never proceeded with, as sufficient information on the concept of a low-powered all-metal fighter had been gained.

Returned to the manufacturers on 12 March 1931, the Vireo had served its purpose and was scrapped not long after.

Technical data – Vireo	
ENGINE	One 230hp supercharged Armstrong Siddeley Lynx IV
WINGSPAN	35ft
LENGTH	27ft 8in
HEIGHT	11ft 5in
WING AREA	214 sq ft
EMPTY WEIGHT	1,951lb
GROSS WEIGHT	2,550lb
MAX SPEED	120mph
SERVICE CEILING	14,750ft

Vickers Type 125 Vireo, N211, at Martlesham Heath, not long after its arrival on 30 March 1928.

Vildebeest Mk I to IV

Development

It was because of a delay in the delivery of the Bristol Beaufort to the RAF that the Vickers Vildebeest, an aircraft dating back to 1928, was to become the only operational torpedo bomber available to Coastal Command in September 1939, and would remain so until April 1940.

The Vildebeest (named Vildebeeste until 1934) was originally designed to specification 24/25, which called for a torpedo bomber to replace the Hawker Horsley introduced in 1927.

Design

The Vildebeest was a large all-metal, fabric-covered single-engined tractor biplane with un-staggered wings. The aircraft followed a similar design pattern to the Vixen family, looking more like a scaled-up version of the Vendace. Vickers' proposal was one of three finally accepted by the Air Ministry to a very specific criteria. The main requirements of 24/25 were a high ceiling and stability to bomb accurately, ability to perform coastal defence and, of course, being able to carry an 18in, 2,000lb torpedo. Planned power, at first, was a Bristol Jupiter VI, but the aircraft was also earmarked for a supercharged Bristol Orion, which never came to fruition. In the end, the prototype was fitted with a 460hp Jupiter VIII, which was loaned from the Air Ministry in November 1927.

Service

The prototype Type 432, serialled N230, was first flown from Brooklands by Tiny Scholefield in April 1928. In September, the aircraft left for Martlesham Heath to compete for 24/25 against the Blackburn Beagle and the Handley Page Hare. The Jupiter VIII suffered badly from cooling problems, but these disappeared when the second prototype was fitted with a Jupiter XFBM. However, the production Vildebeest Mk Is were provided with the 600hp Pegasus IM3.

The Mk I first entered service with 100 Squadron in November 1932, and the following month the first Mk II was ordered with a 635hp Pegasus IIM3 engine. The Mk II was the first version to serve overseas when 100 Squadron was transferred to Singapore in December 1933. The Mk III was a three-seater, the rear cockpit being modified to accommodate the extra crewman. The Vildebeest Mk III was the most prolific version built, 150 of them being delivered to the RAF by the end of 1936. This mark was also the first to serve with another air force when nearly 30 were diverted to the RNZAF, a dozen of these had folding wings and pylons for long-range fuel tanks.

The final variant, the Mk IV, was powered by an 825hp Bristol Perseus driving a three-blade Rotol propeller. The last of 18 ordered were delivered to the RAF by November 1939, although a dozen more were sold to the RNZAF. When the Mk IV joined 42 Squadron in March 1937, it was the first aircraft to join the RAF with a sleeve-valve engine.

The delays to the Beaufort units in the Far East saw two Vildebeest squadrons facing the Japanese alone during the invasion of Singapore in 1941. Heavy losses were inevitable, but the aircraft fought on until the March 1942, when 36 Squadron still had two aircraft on strength.

Production

Total production numbers were as follows: one Type 132 (Jupiter VII); one Type 192 (Jupiter XF); one Type 194 (Jupiter XIF); one Type 204; one Type 209; one Type 214 (Jupiter XFBM); one Type 216 (Hispano-Suiza 12Lbr and floats), 22 Mk Is (Type 244); 30 Mk IIs (Type 258), 150 Mk IIIs (Type 267)

(15 diverted to the RNZAF, including one Mk II); 12 Mk III (Type 277) for RNZAF; 18 Mk IVs for RAF (12 for RNZAF); 26 (Type 245) licence-built Series IX with Hispano-Suiza 12L for the Spanish Navy; and one Type 263 (Pegasus 1M3).

Technical data – Mk I, III & IV	
ENGINE	(I) One 600hp Bristol Pegasus IM3; (III) One 635hp Bristol Pegasus IIM3; (IV) One 825hp Bristol Pegasus VIII
WINGSPAN	49ft
LENGTH	(I & III) 36ft 8in; (IV) 37ft 8in
HEIGHT	14ft 8in
WING AREA	728 sq ft
EMPTY WEIGHT	(I) 4,229lb; (III) 4,773lb; (IV) 4,724lb
GROSS WEIGHT	(I) 8,100lb; (III & IV) 8,500lb
MAX SPEED	(I) 140mph at 10,000ft; (III) 143mph; (IV) 156mph at 5,000ft
ABSOLUTE CEILING	19,000ft
RANGE	(I & III) 1,250 miles at 122mph; (IV) 1,625 miles at 133mph

Right: Originally built as a Vildebeest Mk III, K4164 never entered RAF service but was used instead for a variety of trials until July 1936, when it became the Mk IV prototype, depicted here.

Below: Two Vildebeest prototypes were serialled as N230; this is the second aircraft, fitted with the Jupiter XFBM engine, taxiing at Hendon in June 1932. (*Aeroplane*)

Vellore Mk I to IV

Development

In response to specification 34/24, Vickers outlined the design of a single-engined tractor biplane with the purpose of carrying freight and mail in September 1925. The original plan was for a large (98ft-span) aircraft powered by a Rolls-Royce Condor III engine; the main focus of the machine was its load carrying capability rather than performance, but it was still designed to outrun any land-based equivalent. Vickers submitted a tender for 34/24, which was accepted. The Air Ministry asked that the aircraft be named after an inland town within the British Empire, and the town of Vellore in India was chosen and accepted.

Design

By May 1926, the Air Ministry had moved the goal posts slightly when it requested that a Bristol Jupiter VI engine be used rather than the Condor. The lower-power output of the Jupiter resulted in a smaller aircraft with a span of 74ft, and the all-up-weight was reduced from the Condor's design of 14,000lb to 8,000lb. Another criterion was that the Vellore Mk I (Type 134) should be easy to overhaul and that all major components, including the engine, could be easily accessed and removed if necessary. Even the fabric covering was removable from the all-metal airframe.

The Mk I was later modified with an Armstrong Siddeley Jaguar IV engine specifically for a flight to Australia; the aircraft possibly being redesignated as the Mk II, but definitely being listed as the Type 166.

The Vellore Mk III (Type 172) was a development of the earlier aircraft with a larger cabin and hold capacity, and as a result two engines would be needed. Built at the Crayford works, the Mk III was powered by a pair of Jupiter XIF engines and first appeared as a landplane. A pair of Supermarine-designed floats were later fitted, and the aircraft was presented as a civil mail carrier. A second version, the Mk IV (Type 173), was also built powered by Jupiter IXs with a higher compression ratio than the Mk III.

Service

The Mk I, registered as G-EBYX and with the military serial J8906, was first flown by Scholefield and Payn on 17 May 1928. After a public appearance at Hendon in June and a few modifications, the aircraft was sent to Martlesham Heath for full trials in October. The Vellore performed well for the A&AEE, and the aircraft was described as '... the first aeroplane to go through all its trials without a mechanical failure'. Later fitted with a Jaguar VI engine, G-EBYX was used for an experimental flight to Australia by Flt Lt J. Moir and Fg Off H. C. Owen. After leaving Lympne on 18 March 1929, the engine began playing up over the Mediterranean and again as the duo approached Benghazi. After a forced landing and repairs, the flight resumed on April 28. However, 160 miles off Darwin, the engine began to fail again, but Moir managed to crash-land on Cape Don. The pair praised the aircraft for its handling and comfort over such a long distance.

The Mk III, G-AASW, undertook its maiden flight in the hands of Mutt Summers on 24 June 1930. It took part in that year's King's Cup Air Race, but was unplaced despite averaging 126.8mph. The aircraft was first flown with floats in March 1932 by Supermarine chief test pilot Henri Biard, accompanied by Summers. The Mk IV, registered as G-ABKC, first flew in 1931 as a service type as K2133 and spent most of its time working for the A&AEE, until it was replaced by a Valentia in February 1935.

Technical data – Vellore Mk I & III	
ENGINE	(I) One 515hp Bristol Jupiter IX; (III) Two 525hp Bristol Jupiter XIFs
WINGSPAN	76ft
LENGTH	(I) 51ft 6in; (III) 48ft
HEIGHT	16ft 3in
WING AREA	(I) 1,416 sq ft; (III) 1,373 sq ft
EMPTY WEIGHT	(I) 4,796lb; (III) 7,925lb
GROSS WEIGHT	(I) 9,500lb; (III) 13,000lb
MAX SPEED	(I) 114mph at sea level; (III) 127mph at sea level
RANGE	(I) 350 miles at 80mph; (III) 300 miles

Right: **Vellore Mk III (Type 172) G-AASW during an early test flight, with Mutt Summers at the controls, in 1930. The aircraft was scrapped in 1934.**

Below: **Vellore Mk III G-AASW after a pair of Supermarine-designed floats were attached in early 1932. Henri Biard is in the pilot's seat (right), with Mutt Summers in the co-pilot's position prior to the maiden flight on floats from Southampton Water in March 1932.**

Type 150 B.19/27, Type 163 and Type 255 Vanox

Development

By 1927, serious consideration was already being given to the design of the next generation of bombers to replace the Virginia. Vickers embarked on the project as a private venture, unaware that the Air Ministry was also thinking along the same lines, and, on 17 August 1927, specification B.19/27 was coincidentally issued for a Virginia replacement.

Design

Vickers' original private project was not far from what was required for B.19/27, but the specification demanded a tough set of performance figures, although the bomb load was actually less than the Virginia's. The resulting aircraft was designated as the Type 150, although it was simply referred to as the B.19/27. It was an unequal-span biplane, which incorporated the forward fuselage and tail section of the Virginia, including a new all-moving finless rudder system from the Virginia Mk X. Power was from a pair of Bristol Jupiter VIII engines, but these were later replaced by liquid-cooled Rolls Royce FXIVs.

Following a host of further modifications, the B.19/27 evolved into the Type 255 and was christened the Vanox. The Vickers Type 163 was based upon the Vanox, the aircraft being designed to specification C.16/28, for a troop-transport capable of carrying ten soldiers and equipment over a distance of 1,200 miles. The Type 163 shared many design features with the B.19/27, but could be mainly differentiated by the powerplant, which were four FXVIs, later known as the Kestrel. It could also be a capable bomber, and this aircraft, along with the Type 150 and modified Types 195 and 225, were all entered into the B.19/27 competition.

Service

The B.19/27 (Type 150), serialled J9131, was first flown by Mutt Summers on 30 November, 1929, for just ten minutes from Brooklands. The aircraft began a detailed flight programme, which saw areas of the flight envelope explored and pushed to the limit. Continuous modifications were requested during the flight trials including the fitment of a pair of Pegasus IM3 air-cooled radial engines with Vildebeest propellers. J9131 was trialled by 9 and 10 Squadrons at Boscombe Down including a host of bombing and air gunnery trials but the aircraft, along with the Type 163, ultimately missed out to the Handley Page Heyford and the Fairey Hendon; neither of which fully replaced the Virginia in service.

Technical data – B.19/27 Type 150, Vanox Type 195 & Type 163	
ENGINE	(B.19/27) Two 480hp Rolls-Royce FXIVs (Kestrel); (Vanox) Two 600hp Bristol Pegasus IM3s; (163) Four 480hp Rolls-Royce FXVIs
WINGSPAN	(upper) 76ft 6in; (163) 90ft
LENGTH	(B.19/27) 60ft 6in; (Vanox) 60ft 4in; (163) 66ft 9in
HEIGHT	19ft 3in; (163) 22ft 4in
WING AREA	1,367 sq ft; (163) 1,948 sq ft
GROSS WEIGHT	(B.19/27) 15,400lb; (Vanox) 16,103lb; (163) 25,700lb
MAX SPEED	(B.19/27) 143mph at 12,500ft; (Vanox) 135mph at 5,000ft; (163) 160mph at 6,500ft
SERVICE CEILING	(B.19/27) 23,000ft; (Vanox) 15,000ft; (163) 25,200ft

The Vickers B.19/27 (Type 150) in its original form, at Martlesham Heath, with a pair of Rolls-Royce Kestrel III engines installed. Note the spatted wheels, engine steam condensers and the 2° of sweepback, which was later reduced.

Type 177 (F.21/26)

Development

The one and only Type 177 began as the seventh and final Type 143, which was modified in response to specification N.21/26 for a new single-seat fighter for the Royal Navy. Built as a private venture, the aircraft would find itself up against the Hawker Nimrod, which was not designed to meet 21/26 and N.21/26.

Design

The fuselage of the Type 143 was the only major component of the original aircraft used for the Type 177, which was powered by a Jupiter XF engine driving a four-blade propeller. One novel feature of the Type 177 was that it had steerable hydraulic brakes, which would help to manoeuvre the large biplane on the relatively small aircraft carriers of the day. The big aircraft, which represented the last Vickers single-seat tractor biplane, was not allocated a service serial.

Service

First flown by Mutt Summers from Brooklands on 26 November 1929, it had been delivered to Martlesham Heath for type trials by February 1930. The only issues with the aircraft were an inadequate tail skid, which kept breaking off, and the XF engine, which seized up on March 6 at 20,000ft, but the service pilot managed to force-land with minimal damage to the fin and rudder.

On 1 June 1930, the Type 177 was delivered to Gosport in preparation for deck-landing trials aboard HMS *Furious*. As good an idea as the steerable brakes were, all service pilots who flew the Type 177 found them very difficult to get used to, and on 11 June the biplane was put on its nose, destroying the four-blade propeller. This was immediately replaced by a spare two-blade propeller, and trials continued either without using the brakes or by a delicate application of them. The use of the new propeller also upset the firing of the Type 177s twin Vickers machine guns, which were dependent on gun-control gear, and its timing could be easily upset.

In the end, the Type 177 and all of the other entrants to the 21/26 or N.21/26 competition, which included the Armstrong Whitworth Starling II and XVI, Blackburn Blackcock, Fairey Firefly III, Gloster Gnatsnapper, Hawker Hoopoe and Parnall Pipit, were found to be unsuitable for the specification. However, the Hawker Nimrod, which had specification 16/30 written for it, was accepted in numbers into Royal Navy service.

The Type 177 was later considered for a more powerful Armstrong Siddeley Panther or Jaguar engine. Only the latter is believed to have been briefly fitted, but no performance figures exist to support the fact.

Technical data – Type 177	
ENGINE	One 540hp Bristol Jupiter XFS
WINGSPAN	34ft 3in
LENGTH	27ft 6in
HEIGHT	11ft 3in
WING AREA	336 sq ft
EMPTY WEIGHT	2,835lb
GROSS WEIGHT	4,050lb
MAX SPEED	190mph at 13,120ft
ABSOLUTE CEILING	30,000ft
RANGE	470 miles at 175mph and 15,000ft

The Vickers Type 177 at Martlesham Heath, prior to flight trials commencing in February 1930.

Jockey Mk I
(Type 151 and 171) aka
Vickers Interceptor

Development

By the late 1920s, British strategists, quite rightly, predicted that one of the main tasks for fighter aircraft would be to intercept fast, high-flying bombers. Thank goodness that this was recognised ten years before the next world war, because the outcome of the Battle of Britain could have been so different. The Air Ministry's requirements were quite simple; it needed an aircraft that was very quick and could climb to height in the shortest possible time. This was encompassed in specification F.20/27 for an interception single-seater day fighter, capable of reaching an enemy aircraft flying at 20,000ft and a speed of 150mph. The latter figure would be shattered within a short space of time with the arrival of the Fairey Fox bomber.

Design

Designed to designation Type 151 and named the Jockey, the aircraft was conceived by Rex Pierson and J. Bewsher and, as per the specification, was to be powered by a Bristol Mercury IIA radial engine, which was rated at 480hp at 13,000ft. The name Jockey was unofficial, but it was used in an effort to attract the French to the project as it was a nickname for all single-seat fighters in France at the time.

The Type 151 was built using the Vickers-Wibault all-metal construction system in a similar fashion to the Vireo. Bewsher, who had previously been employed as a consultant designer by Vickers, spent much of his time selecting the right wing for the Type 151, and at one stage the Wibault W116 section was considered. Ultimately, the finished aircraft adopted a parallel chord of thick RAF-34 airfoil (the same as the Viastra), which eliminated internal and external bracing.

The Jockey was redesignated as the Type 171 when a Jupiter VIIF engine was installed. However, under specification F.5/34, another Vickers' aircraft was initially referred to as the Jockey Mk II, but it was subsequently renamed as the Venom (Type 279). Construction of the Jockey Mk III (Type 196) was started, but never completed, although the aircraft was registered as G-AAWG in April 1933.

Service

The first flight of the Jockey Mk I, now serialled as J9122, broke with tradition as the aircraft was transported by road to Martlesham Heath. Once there, the Mercury IIA engine, which was the property of the Air Ministry, was fitted, and the little fighter undertook its maiden flight in April 1930. The aircraft experienced a vibration in the rear fuselage during early flight testing, which was cured when the internal bracing was redesigned by Barnes Wallis.

Further improvements such as a Townend ring around the engine and spats around the wheels helped to increase the performance of the Jockey. This was further improved when a 530hp Jupiter VIIF was installed, but the full potential of the Jockey was never realised because the aircraft was lost in a flat spin on 15 July 1932. The aircraft was successfully abandoned by the pilot at 5,000ft near Woodbridge.

Technical data – Jockey Mk I	
ENGINE	One 480hp Bristol Mercury IIA replaced by one 530hp Bristol Jupiter VIIF
WINGSPAN	32ft 6in
LENGTH	23ft
HEIGHT	8ft 3in
WING AREA	150 sq ft
EMPTY WEIGHT	2,260lb
GROSS WEIGHT	3,161lb
MAX SPEED	218mph at 10,000ft
ABSOLUTE CEILING	31,000ft

This is Jockey J9122 after the fighter was modified with a drag-reducing Townend ring around the original Mercury engine and wheel spats. The aircraft was armed with a pair of .303in Vickers machine guns.

Viastra Mk I to IV and VIII to X

Development

In the spring of 1928, Vickers found itself studying a specification for a new ten-seat commercial monoplane that could be powered by a single Bristol Jupiter IX or a trio of Armstrong Siddeley Lynx IVs. The specification was accompanied by an in-depth market survey of airlines across the world, which would see the Vickers' sales strategy focusing on regions where surface transport had not yet reached the same standards as Europe.

Design

A high-wing monoplane design was eventually chosen with a pair of cabane-mounted engines under each wing and a third in the nose. The all-metal Type 160 Viastra Mk I was powered by three 270hp Lynx Major engines. The aircraft was influenced by many Wibault features, such as the way the fuselage was constructed and the external metal skin that also covered the wing. The Viastra was built at the Supermarine Aviation Works at Woolston under the guidance of Trevor Westbrook from Weybridge.

The Mk II (Type 198) had a 12-seat capacity, and two of them, powered by a pair of Jupiter XIF engines, were built specifically for West Australian Airways (WAA). The Mk III (Type 199) was the Mk I converted to take a pair of Jaguar VIc engines, while the Mk VI (Type 203) was a freighter version powered by a single Jupiter XIF. The Mk VIII (Type 220) was the Mk III converted again with three Jupiter VIFM engines, the Mk IX (Type 242) was fitted with Jupiter IXF engines and the Mk X (Type 259) was a VIP conversion powered by a pair of Pegasus IIL3 engines. A final version, named the Wallis-Viastra (Type 256), was built with a geodetic wing, but is believed not to have flown.

Service

Once completed, the Viastra Mk I, G-AAUB, was towed from the Supermarine works to the river Itchen, where it was loaded onto a lighter and transported to the nearby Hamble aerodrome. On 1 October 1930, the aircraft completed its maiden flight in the hands of Mutt Summers. The two Viastra Mk IIs built, served as VH-UOO and VH-UOM, respectively, with WAA, as replacements for the company's ageing DH.66 Hercules aircraft. VH-UOM was written off in a landing accident at a staging post in October 1933, and VH-UOO was retired when Australian National Airways took over WAA in 1936.

No sales were achieved for the Mk III or VIII, and the aircraft served as demonstrators, while the seven-seat VIP Mk X did give some service. First registered as G-ACCC in December 1932, the aircraft joined the King's Flight and was allocated for the specific use of the Prince of Wales, who did not use the aircraft very much. It was later used by the Air Ministry for flight testing radio equipment and was then passed on to Imperial Airways to train its radio operators. This luxurious aircraft was dismantled in 1937.

Technical data – Viastra Mk I & II	
ENGINE	(I) Three Armstrong Siddeley Lynx Xs; (II) Two 525hp Bristol Jupiter XIFs
WINGSPAN	70ft
LENGTH	45ft 6in
HEIGHT	13ft 6in
WING AREA	745 sq ft
EMPTY WEIGHT	7,880lb
GROSS WEIGHT	12,350lb
MAX SPEED	120mph at sea level
RANGE	535 miles

The sole Viastra Mk VI (Type 203) freighter, marked '0-6' and powered by a single Jupiter XIF engine. The Viastra freighter failed to secure any commercial orders.

COW Gun Fighter

Development

Several attempts, both during and since the end of World War One, had been made to design an aircraft capable of carrying a high-calibre weapon, which could knock an enemy aircraft out of the sky with a single round. The idea was resurrected by the Air Ministry when they issued specification F.29/27 for an interceptor to be built around the 37mm COW (Coventry Ordnance Works) gun, which could fire 1½lb shells. The rest of the specification was similar to the earlier 20/27, which required the interceptor to be powerful enough to tackle an enemy bomber flying at 20,000ft and 150mph.

Design

Vickers' response to F.29/27 was to look at its own history books and design an aircraft in the single-seat pusher configuration, in a similar vein to its World War One F.B.12 and F.B.26. The COW Gun Fighter (Type 161), at first glance, certainly had a World War One look about it, but under the skin the aircraft incorporated the latest construction techniques and many novel features. For example, the aircraft's control cables were concealed within the tubular tail booms rather than being exposed. The wings, which were of RAF-34 section, were high-aspect-ratio and made of duralumin plate with a tubular structure covered in fabric. These helped to give the fighter a respectable climb rate. The aircraft was also fitted with adjustable in-flight elevator trim-tabs, quite possibly the first machine to have them.

The COW gun, which weighed 200lb, was mounted in the nose of the aircraft immediately opposite the pilot so that it was within his reach. Positioned at an angle of 45°, the COW had 50 shells, which loaded automatically. The weapon was targeted through a periscope, mounted on the left-hand side of the pilot's dashboard. Power was intended to be a Mercury IIA, but, prior to the maiden flight, a 530hp Jupiter VIIF was fitted instead.

Service

It was only the intention of the Vickers' designers to see the COW Gun Fighter, serialled J9566, taxied on 21 January 1931, but test pilot Mutt Summers obviously had complete faith in the machine and decided to carry out a short maiden flight instead. After some minor adjustments, the aircraft was sent to Martlesham Heath for evaluation in September 1931.

Other than a few very minor problems, which were easily rectified, the COW Gun Fighter performed exceptionally well at Martlesham, and all who flew the machine had nothing but praise for it but no orders came, and the idea was tucked away again. The concept of an upward-firing heavy calibre weapon served the Luftwaffe well when it introduced the deadly Schräge Musik against Bomber Command during World War Two. Possibly yet another opportunity was missed by the senior staff of the Air Ministry.

Technical data – COW Gun Fighter	
ENGINE	One 530hp Bristol Jupiter VIIF
WINGSPAN	32ft
LENGTH	23ft 6in
HEIGHT	12ft 4in
WING AREA	270 sq ft
EMPTY WEIGHT	2,381lb
GROSS WEIGHT	3,350lb
MAX SPEED	185mph at 10,000ft
CLIMB RATE	10,000ft in 5.8mins

The striking COW Gun Fighter, J9566, was ordered as an interceptor specifically to carry the 37mm gun. The long fairing running from the centre of the engine to tail was an experimental design, on behalf of the National Physical Laboratory, to see if it improved stability and top speed.

Vincent

Development
Prompted by specification G.4/31 for a new general-purpose aircraft, Rex Pierson decided in 1931 to design a conversion of the Vildebeest. This would entail converting the coastal torpedo bomber into an aircraft capable of carrying out those duties being placed upon the RAF in the Middle East, ground support and light bombing.

Design
The one problem that the RAF crews had been suffering from in the Middle East was a lack of range, which was not ideal with the vast and remote environment they were flying over, especially when coupled with a distinct shortage of suitable landing grounds.

Once the Vildebeest's torpedo equipment was removed there was room for a 100-gallon fuel tank below the fuselage, which would extend the new aircraft's range to 1,250 miles. The big Vildebeest was also ideal to accommodate the large amount of service equipment demanded of G.4/31 as a well as being capable of carrying a 1,056lb bomb load, desert survival equipment, a wireless and a message pick-up hook.

Once Pierson presented his ideas, the Air Ministry accepted all of the proposals in principle and agreed that one Vildebeest Mk I, S1714, would be used as a prototype. The aircraft would be powered with the engine of the Vildebeest Mk III, the Bristol IIM.3. S1714, and it undertook its maiden flight on 24 November 1932. Within a month, it was being shipped off to Egypt for service trials entailing an assessment by all RAF general purpose squadrons located in the Middle East and North Africa. On return to England, a new specification, No. 21/33, was produced around Pierson's design, and in late 1933 a production order for 51 aircraft was placed. It was only in 1934 that the name Vincent was applied to the aircraft.

Service
With the exception of the first production aircraft, which was retained in the UK for various trials, all Vincents were shipped to the Middle East, the first of them joining 84 Squadron in December 1934. 8 Squadron followed in February 1935, a unit which was destined to operate the Vincent until March 1942. These two units alone took delivery of 46 aircraft.

As production orders increased, 45 Squadron was re-equipped in November 1935, and both 47 and 207 squadrons, operating in the Sudan, received Vincents in 1936. By the outbreak of World War Two, only 8 and 47 squadrons were still fully equipped with the type, although a new unit, 244 Squadron, was formed at Shaibah with Vincents in November 1940. The latter unit saw action against the Iraqi Army in May 1941, when the RAF station at Habbaniya was threatened. 244 Squadron was also destined to be the last Vincent unit until fully re-equipped with Blenheims in January 1943.

Production
In total, 197 Vincents were built: K4105–K4155 (four of this batch supplied to New Zealand and one to Iraq); K4615–K4619 (one to New Zealand); K4656 –K4750 (17 to New Zealand and three to Iraq); K4883–K4885 and K6326–K6368.

Technical data – Vincent	
ENGINE	One 635hp Bristol Pegasus IIM3
WINGSPAN	49ft
LENGTH	36ft 8in
HEIGHT	17ft 9in
WING AREA	728 sq ft
EMPTY WEIGHT	4,229lb
GROSS WEIGHT	8,100lb
MAX SPEED	142mph at 5,000ft
SERVICE CEILING	19,000ft
RANGE	1,250 miles at 133mph

Vincent K4687 was one of a batch of 95 delivered to the RAF between September 1935 and February 1936. This aircraft was serving with 47 Squadron on 14 February 1938 when it flew into the ground between Khartoum and Es Sufeiya. (Charles E. Brown)

M.1/30

Development

March 1930 saw the issue of specification M.1/30 for a replacement for the carrier-borne Blackburn Ripon torpedo bomber. This coincided with the liquidation of the AGC, which had produced the R.100; the staff of the company being allowed to go their separate ways, although Barnes Wallis decided to join Rex Pierson at Weybridge as chief structures designer.

Design

Power was crucial for the new torpedo bomber, and Vickers choose the new geared and moderately supercharged 825hp Rolls-Royce H10 engine, which was later renamed the Buzzard IIIMS. The new aircraft, which was simply referred to as the M.1/30 and given the designation Type 207, was a big conventional looking tractor biplane. The aircraft was to be produced with all relevant service equipment installed, such as a radio, electrical services, wheel brakes, hoisting-gear attachments and an arrester hook. The M.1/30 also featured Frise-type ailerons, Handley Page slots and wings that folded rearwards for carrier operations.

The experience Wallis had gained during the construction of the R.100 influenced the general arrangement of the M.1/30. The wing spars were made in the same way as airship members and so was the construction of the fuselage.

The undercarriage was a split-axle type, so that a torpedo could be carried between the legs. The angle of the torpedo could be adjusted on the ground depending on the water-running characteristic required. As a standard bomber, the M.1/30 could carry a single 2,000lb bomb or one 1,000lb and four 500lb bombs below the central lower inner wing. A single .303in Lewis machine gun was mounted in the rear cockpit for self-defence.

Service

Serialled S1641, the M.1/30 was first flown from Brooklands on 11 January 1933, with Mutt Summers at the controls and John Radcliffe as his flight observer. Twenty-four test flights were made over the coming months; the majority were only short, as various minor modifications were carried out, such as changing the position of the mass balances for the control surfaces. The introduction of a 2° dihedral into the upper main plane was the only major change, however. On 23, November 1933, Summers and Radcliffe took off to perform an altitude and level speed trial with a full war load, including an unarmed torpedo. The engine was running a little rough during the flight, and Summers decided to break from the original flight plan and proceed with a high-speed dive test. Summers pushed the nose gently down to an angle of 45°, which saw the airspeed rise to 200kts. Suddenly, after a further slight increase in speed, the nose came up slightly, and the starboard wing structure began to fail before the M.1/30 entered a violent uncontrolled half-roll. The fuselage became detached, throwing Summers clear, his parachute opening immediately while Radcliffe remained for a few agonised seconds with his parachute back-strap caught on the machine gun. Radcliffe eventually managed to detach himself as the M.1/30 showered itself across the countryside. The cause was put down to tailplane failure, and as a result neither the Vickers M.1/30 nor the other entrants to the competition were chosen as a Ripon replacement.

Technical data – M.1/30	
ENGINE	One 825hp Rolls-Royce Buzzard IIIMS
WINGSPAN	50ft
LENGTH	43ft 7in
HEIGHT	14ft 5in
WING AREA	724 sq ft
EMPTY WEIGHT	5,200lb
GROSS WEIGHT	9,600lb
MAX SPEED	159mph at 4,000ft
CLIMB RATE	4,000ft in 5 mins
SERVICE CEILING	16,000ft

The Vickers M.1/30 was designed as a replacement for the Blackburn Ripon torpedo bomber. Built to specification M.1/30, none of the aircraft submitted by Vickers, Blackburn (M.1/30) or Handley Page (H.P.46) were chosen.

Vellox

Development

A development of the Vickers Vellore, the one and only Type 212 Vellox, was designed as a long-haul passenger carrying aircraft. All attempts by Vickers to tempt the Air Ministry to order the Vellox as a troop-carrying aircraft failed, mainly because it was being presented with the same engines that powered its intended replacement, the Victoria V.

Design

The Vellox was originally being built as the third-production Vellore Mk III. Vickers redesigned the aircraft, which included rebuilding the fuselage with a much larger cabin. This idea was originally proposed by the Air Ministry, which ordered a mail-carrying version of the Vellore instead. Using bits from the part-built Mk III, the Vellox slowly emerged, although it was to be named the Victrix originally.

Initial efforts to market the Vellox with Jupiter XFBM engines, as per the Victoria Mk V, failed, and a pair of moderately supercharged Pegasus IM3s were used instead. The Vellox was operated by a crew of two plus a steward who looked after ten passengers; alternatively, 3,000lbs of freight could be carried once the seats were removed. The Vellox also introduced ventilation for its passengers via a ram air intake mounted on top of the fuselage, as well as soundproofing, full galley and toilet facilities and stressed seating complete with rubber sponge upholstery.

From an engineering point of the view, the aircraft was fitted with inertia-type starters, pneumatic wheel brakes, de-icing equipment and electrical instrumentation.

Service

In the hands of Mutt Summers, the aircraft took to the air from Brooklands on 23 January 1934. Two days later, the aircraft was delivered to Martlesham Heath for civil type tests. The aircraft was only criticised for some vibration at cruising speed, which was later cured by fitting a pair of four-bladed propellers from the Supermarine Southampton X flying-boat. It also suffered from a low cruising speed once all of the extras were installed in the Vellox.

Still, no interest came from the military or civilian marketplace, and the sole aircraft, registered as G-ABKY back in March 1931, remained a Vickers aircraft until May 1936 when it was sold to Imperial Airways. The airline operated the aircraft as a freighter, but found it to have too low a cruising speed, which was not improved when a pair of Pegasus IIL engines were fitted. Vickers blamed the poor performance on extra equipment that had been fitted, and this factor may have contributed to the aircraft's demise on 10 August 1936. Whilst taking off from Croydon Airport bound for Paris at night, the Vellox crashed into Hillside Gardens, killing all four crew; the cause was blamed on engine failure.

Technical data – Vellox	
ENGINE	Two 600hp Bristol Pegasus IM3s
WINGSPAN	76ft
LENGTH	50ft 6in
HEIGHT	16ft 3in
WING AREA	1,374 sq ft
EMPTY WEIGHT	8,150lb
GROSS WEIGHT	13,500lb
MAX SPEED	157mph at 6,500ft
RANGE	690 miles at 133mph

The one and only Vickers Type 212 Vellox, witnessed just prior to its maiden flight at Brooklands in January 1934. The aircraft had a protracted existence, which saw it cheaply sold off to Imperial Airways in May 1936, only to be destroyed in an accident near Croydon a few months later.

G.4/31 Biplane

Development

Another chance for Barnes Wallis to shine came in November 1931, when Vickers tendered three different designs for specification G.4/31, which sought a new general-purpose and torpedo aircraft. The Air Ministry favoured an air-cooled Bristol Pegasus IM3 engine for the specification, which featured in two of the Vickers designs. These were for an open cockpit, low-wing monoplane with a fixed trousered undercarriage, powered by IM3; a Rolls-Royce Kestrel IIIM water-cooled version of the previous monoplane and a big-span Pegasus-powered biplane, which, on the surface, looked similar to the Vespa. After examination by the ministry, the latter was accepted, and a contract was issued for a single aircraft in 1932.

Design

While work began on the G.4/31 (Type 253), Wallis also made a start on the monoplane design as a private venture, which would run in parallel with the biplane. This had a fuselage completely designed by Wallis, with four very light-weight longerons built in sections with screwed joints, in much simpler fashion to the M.1/30. Around the longerons were entwined spiral channel members in opposing directions, which formed a lattice structure.

The wings were more conventional, using an RAF-34 (later changed to the thicker RAF-15) wing section with twin spars and a pair of struts to each bay. Both wings were fitted with ailerons, and the upper was fitted with leading edge slats. A split-axle undercarriage was used to give ample space for a torpedo. Power was provided by a Pegasus IIM3 nine-cylinder, single-row, air-cooled radial engine.

Service

Serialled as K2771, the G.4/31 was first flown from Brooklands on 16 August 1934. A variety of experimental modifications followed, some were for Vickers' benefit and others for the RAE at Farnborough, before the aircraft was delivered to Martlesham Heath for service trials. By February 1935, the big biplane had been re-engined with a Pegasus IIIM3 powerplant, and an order for 150 aircraft was placed by the Air Ministry. Simultaneously, the G.4/31 monoplane was in the air, and comparative trials between the two revealed that the monoplane was significantly better in all areas. As a result, the order for a biplane was cancelled, and only one example was ever built.

Following further engine assessments with the RAE in August 1936, the aircraft was transferred to Bristol's at Filton for engine development trials. On 22 February 1941, the aircraft was moved to 50 MU at Cowley until it was SOC on 19 April 1941 and given the instructional airframe number 2574M.

Technical data – G.4/31	
ENGINE	One 635hp Bristol Pegasus IIM3
WINGSPAN	52ft 7in
LENGTH	37ft
HEIGHT	12ft 6in
WING AREA	579 sq ft
EMPTY WEIGHT	4,500lb
GROSS WEIGHT	8,350lb
MAX SPEED	161mph at 4,500ft

The Vickers G.4/31 biplane, K2771, taxiing at the RAF Display, Hendon, in June 1935. It was at this show that the particulars of the G.4/31 biplane and monoplane were publicly compared on display boards for all to see, determining that the monoplane was the way forward.

K2771 is at Martlesham Heath for official trials, having already been assessed by the Royal Aircraft Establishment (RAE) at Farnborough. An order for 150 G.4/31 biplanes was placed by the Air Ministry, only to be cancelled not long after in favour of the PV monoplane, aka, the Vickers Wellesley.

G.4/31 Monoplane and Wellesley Mk I

Development

The first aircraft to join the RAF with geodetic construction was the Vickers Wellesley light bomber. Although the aircraft was obsolete by the beginning of World War Two in the European theatre, it was successfully employed in East Africa, Egypt and the Middle East.

Design

As described in the chapter on the G.4/31 biplane, the monoplane was being designed simultaneously as a private venture by Barnes Wallis. While the biplane was a good aircraft in its own right, the Type 246 monoplane totally outperformed it, so the planned contract for 150 biplanes was cancelled, and a total of 177 Type 287 Wellesleys were ordered instead. The Type 256 was first flown by Mutt Summers on 19 June 1935, but, in defence of the biplane, the monoplane did not meet all of the general-purpose requirements of the original specification, and was ordered as a pure bomber aircraft. To accommodate the monoplane, specification 22/25 was written for the aircraft.

Service

The Wellesley first entered service with 76 Squadron at Finningley in April 1937, and as the RAF expanded, five further squadrons were equipped with the type. By April 1939, the Wellesley was already being replaced by Battles, Hampdens and Whitleys, but rather than withdrawing the light bomber completely, 100 were transferred to units in the Middle East. The first of these was 45 Squadron in November 1937, followed by 223 Squadron in June 1938 and 47 Squadron in 1939; all had flown the Vickers Vincent.

The Wellesley first went into action in East Africa against the Italians as part of 254 Wing (14, 47 and 223 squadrons). On the first day of the East African campaign, Wellesleys of 14 Squadron bombed Massawa, while 223 Squadron successfully attacked Addis Ababa on 18 August 1940. The Wellesley was later used in the region for shipping reconnaissance patrols, the last examples serving with 47 Squadron until August 1943.

The one event that the Wellesley achieved notoriety for was when three aircraft, L2638, L2639 and L2680 of the RAF's Long-Range Development Flight, captured the World Long-Distance Record in November 1938. Led by Sqn Ldr Richard Kellett, the trio took off from Ismailia in Egypt on 5 November and flew non-stop to Darwin, Australia, a distance of 7,162 miles, in just over 48 hours. L2639 had to land at Kupang before crossing the Timor Sea, leaving the two remaining aircraft to capture the record.

Production

In total, 176 Wellesleys (Type 287s) were built (including the prototype) in the serial ranges K7713–K7791 (79), K8520–K8536 (17) and L2637–L2716 (80), all delivered between 4 March 1937 and 30 May 1938.

Technical data – G.4/31 & Wellesley Mk I	
ENGINE	(G.4/31) One 680hp Bristol Pegasus IIIM3; (Mk I) One 925hp Pegasus XX; (Distance Record) One Pegasus XXII
WINGSPAN	74ft 7in
LENGTH	39ft 3in
HEIGHT	12ft 4in
WING AREA	630 sq ft
EMPTY WEIGHT	6,812lb
GROSS WEIGHT	11,128lb
MAX SPEED	222mph at 15,000ft
SERVICE CEILING	26,100ft
RANGE	1,100 miles

The Wellesley pre-production prototype, K7556, which was built to new specification 22/35, flies for the first time from Brooklands on 15 June 1935. The aircraft went on to spend most of its time with the RAE and the A&AEE until it was struck off charge (SOC) in March 1940.

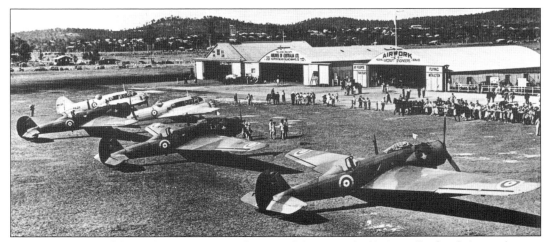

All three Wellesleys of the RAF's Long-Range Development Flight are reunited in Australia after their record-breaking flight in November 1938. The aircraft are about to commence a tour of Australia after breaking the World Long-Distance Record.

Venom

Development

By the mid-1930s, the performance difference between the bomber and the fighter was rapidly narrowing, and potential heights at which defenders and attackers would engage was increasing. Specification F.5/34 was issued for such an aircraft, with a heavy armament of eight Browning machine guns.

Design

Vickers' approach to F.5/34 was to redesign the Jockey with a 625hp Aquila AE-3S sleeve-valve engine, trimmed off with an NACA cowling. The engine was hinged, which gave excellent access to the unit during servicing and general maintenance. The new fighter had many advanced features, such as 90° deflection trailing-edge flaps, an electric undercarriage and a high-lift wing. A 12v generator provided power for gun heating, the engine starter, all aircraft lights, an undercarriage warning horn, reflector-sight illumination, flap and undercarriage retraction and the radio.

The aircraft was constructed of metal with an exceptionally smooth exterior, which was achieved by a stressed skin held in place by countersunk rivets. The full armament of eight .303in Browning machine guns was in place from the start, and these were accessed via large removable panels.

Service

Prior to its maiden flight, the Vickers F.5/34 was named the Venom (Type 279) and given the company test serial PVO-10. On 17 June 1936, Mutt Summers took the Venom aloft for the first time from Brooklands, having already flown the inline water-cooled Spitfire prototype three months earlier. The Hurricane was also already in production, and the odds were obviously stacked against the radial powered Venom from the start. There was no sign of a radial engine at that time coming anywhere near matching the power of the Rolls-Royce PV12, which would later be known as the Merlin.

Extensive manufacturer's trials were carried out by Flt Lt J. K. Quill, who had just joined Vickers from the RAF. Quill conducted many Venom test flights from Eastleigh in harmony with the test programme that he was also carrying out with the Spitfire.

Prior to being delivered to Martlesham Heath, the Venom was fitted with another novel feature for the day, a tail parachute for spinning tests. These were never performed because, on arrival at Martlesham, the aircraft spent more time on the ground than in the air due to engine and ancillary problems.

The Venom was an excellent attempt to create a high-performance fighter using a relatively low-powered radial engine, but it would have always lagged behind the Hurricane and Spitfire. It was, however, very manoeuvrable, having an exceptionally tight turning radius and a good rate of roll.

Technical data – Venom	
ENGINE	One 625hp Bristol Aquila AE-3S
WINGSPAN	32ft 9in
LENGTH	24ft 2in
HEIGHT	10ft 9in
WING AREA	146 sq ft
GROSS WEIGHT	4,156lb
MAX SPEED	312mph at 16,250ft
CLIMB RATE	3,000 ft/min
SERVICE CEILING	32,000ft

The Vickers F.5/34, later named the Venom, was a good attempt at producing a high-performance fighter with a radial engine. However, the aircraft was on the back foot from the start, with the Hurricane and Spitfire arriving on the scene before the aircraft first flew in June 1936.

Wellington Prototype

Development

It was October 1932 when Vickers placed a tender for specification B.9/32 for a twin-engined medium bomber. A great deal was made of the fact that the B.9/32 would make full use of geodetics, a technique that had already proved itself to be the strongest method of construction being practised at the time, and endorsed during structural tests by the RAE at Farnborough. As a result of the potential strength of the airframe alone, the Air Ministry ordered a single Type 271 prototype.

Design

Thanks to the perseverance of Rex Pierson and Gustav Lachmann of Handley Page (which was also tendering for B.9/32), the traditional process of making manufacturers stick to the tare weight laid down in the original specification was lifted from June 1934. This allowed the designers the freedom to choose whatever powerplant was available. A good example of this is, when the B.9/32 tender was submitted in 1933, the aircraft had to weigh 6,300lb, but, by the time the prototype flew, it had risen to 11,508lb. This autonomy was not available to aircraft designers prior to B.9/32, and, as a result of its introduction, more appropriate aircraft began to enter service.

The B.9/32 was virtually designed in response to world events, beginning in 1932 when the Geneva Conference of Disarmament sought to impose a tare weight limit of 6,500lb on all bombers. Evidently, Germany and Italy had a different idea, and the proposals from the conference were soon dismissed as an arms race began. The Wellington, which was originally called the Crecy before it was renamed after the Duke of Wellington, would be at the forefront of this race and would provide the backbone for Bomber Command, which, at first, struggled to find its feet.

Service

Serialled K4049, the prototype B.9/32 was first flown by Mutt Summers on 15 June 1936, and within days it was on public display at Hendon. The aircraft only bore a passing resemblance to the future Wellington, as it appeared with no turrets and a tail, which was 'borrowed' from a Supermarine Stranraer flying-boat. The powerplant changed many times thanks to the looser specification, the prototype being fitted with the latest 915hp Bristol Pegasus X engines.

The aircraft was designed for a crew of four, plus room for a fifth for special duties. The potential bomb load was nine 500lb bombs, or nine 250lb bombs for long-range operations. Although not fitted, defensive armament would have been light, with a single .303in machine gun in the nose and another in the tail.

Being declared as one of the most advanced aircraft of the day, a claim that was supported by excellent test reports from the A&AEE, justified an order being placed for 180 Mk Is in 1935. However, the full flight programme of K4049 was destined never to be completed, as the aircraft was lost on 19 April 1937, after a horn balance failed over Brightwell, Suffolk. The pilot was thrown clear as the bomber turned onto its back, but the only other occupant, the flight engineer, was unable to escape before the aircraft hit the ground.

Technical data – Wellington Prototype	
ENGINE	Two 915hp Bristol Pegasus Xs
WINGSPAN	86ft
LENGTH	61ft 3in
HEIGHT	17ft 5in
WING AREA	840 sq ft
EMPTY WEIGHT	18,000lb
GROSS WEIGHT	24,850lb
MAX SPEED	250mph at 8,000ft
SERVICE CEILING	21,600ft
RANGE	3,200 miles

The prototype B.9/32, K4049, at Hendon only days after completing its maiden flight from Brooklands on 15 June 1936. The aircraft was called the Crecy at the time of this photograph, but within two months was renamed the Wellington, after the Duke of Wellington, in keeping with the naming of the Wellesley, which was the Duke's family name. *(Aeroplane)*

Wellington Mk I, IA, IC and GR Mk VIII

Development
The Wellington had been prepared for massed production even before the B.9/32 prototype had flown. The production aircraft differed from the original machine by a considerable margin, and many considered the first production Mk I as the true Wellington prototype.

Design
The Wellington Mk I (Type 290) was initially powered by a pair of 915hp Pegasus X engines when L4212, the first of a batch of 180 aircraft ordered in 1935, undertook its maiden flight on 23 December 1937. Designed to a new specification, 29/36, the Mk I was fitted with three power-operated Vickers' turrets, each containing a pair of .303in machine guns. In service, the Mk I was powered by a pair 1,050hp Pegasus XVIII engines, giving the aircraft the ability to carry a bomb load of 4,000lb, which was three times more than the Handley Page Heyford.

The Mk IA was actually meant to be built as the Mk II, and one of its features was the ability to accept a Pegasus or Merlin powerplant. In the end, the idea was not pursued, and the mark was only fitted with the Pegasus X. The troublesome Vickers' turrets were also replaced with Fraser-Nash turrets. FN5 turrets were fitted into the nose and tail, while an FN25 replaced the Vickers unit in the ventral position; each was fitted with a pair of .303in machine guns. The all-up weight of the Mk IA increased to 28,000lb, and the undercarriage was strengthened and slightly repositioned to cope with it.

The Mk IB was a back-up solution to the Wellington's gun turret problems, which were rectified with the Mk IA. Any Mk IBs built were quickly redesignated to Mk IAs.

The Mk IC was produced in great numbers, but only differed from the Mk IA by having the ventral turret removed and replaced with a pair of .303in machine guns positioned in each of the rear fuselage windows. Initially, these were Vickers 'K' guns, but the majority built were supplied with a pair of belt-fed .303in Browning machine guns. The Mk IC was also fitted with much improved hydraulics.

Service
The Mk I first joined 99 Squadron at Mildenhall in October 1938, and by the beginning of the war eight operational units (plus two in reserve) were equipped with the Wellington, all of them within 3 Group. Mainly because of its weak and unreliable defensive armament, the Mk I was phased out of RAF service in favour of the Fraser-Nash equipped Mk IA from December 1939.

The Mk IC was the early mainstay, the type re-equipping squadrons from April 1940 and remaining in production until late 1942.

Production
In total, 185 Mk Is, 183 Mk IAs and 2,684 Mk ICs were built between 1936 and 1942 at Weybridge, Blackpool and Chester. Additionally, 395 Mk ICs were converted to GR Mk VIII standard for Coastal Command.

Technical data – Wellington Mk I, IC	
ENGINE	(I & IC) Two 1,050hp Bristol Pegasus XVIIIs
WINGSPAN	(I) 86ft; (IC) 86ft 2in
LENGTH	(I) 61ft 3in; (IC) 64ft 7in
HEIGHT	17ft 5in
WING AREA	840 sq ft
EMPTY WEIGHT	(I) 18,000lb; (IC) 18,556lb
GROSS WEIGHT	(I) 24,850lb; (IC) 28,500lb
MAX SPEED	(I) 245mph at 15,000ft; (IC) 235mph at 15,500ft
CLIMB RATE	15,000ft in 18 mins
SERVICE CEILING	(I) 21,600ft; (IC) 18,000ft

Above left: The first production Vickers Wellington was Mk I L4212, which was initially flown in December 1937. After tours of duty with A&AEE, RAE, 2 GRU and 3 GRU, the aircraft served until 1 January 1942, when it was wrecked in a forced landing at Edwinstowe, Nottinghamshire.

Above right: A three-ship of Wellington Mk Is of 149 Squadron, north of Thetford in Norfolk. As part of 3 Group, 149 Squadron re-equipped with Wellingtons, replacing the Heyford, in January 1939, and operated the type until November 1941, when the four-engine Stirling took over.

One of the most famous Wellingtons preserved today is also the only example of a complete Mk IA. N2890 was built at Weybridge in November 1939, and, after surviving several early operations, the aircraft served with 20 Operational Training Unit (OUT). On 31 December 1940, the aircraft was ditched in Loch Ness, where it remained until successfully recovered in September 1985.

Wellington Mk II

Development

The design of the Wellington Mk II began in January 1938 with the Rolls-Royce Merlin X engine. The change of powerplant would enable production of the aircraft to remain uninterrupted, if the supply of the Pegasus should fail through technical problems or, more likely, due to enemy action.

Design

The Mk II was not just an aircraft with a different powerplant, which, incidentally, would not become available until 1939, it was also fitted with Fraser-Nash turrets, and a 24v electrical system was installed for both aircraft and radio services. The hydraulic system was upgraded with VSG type pumps, which supplied up to 1,000lb/sq in power supply for all aircraft services plus 300lb/sq into a secondary system that powered the turrets. The oxygen system was also modified to suit the Fraser-Nash turrets. All of these upgrades were incorporated into the Mk IA and IC before the Mk II even flew, because no Merlin engine was available.

By early 1939, the Merlin X engine was ready for testing and on 3 March the Mk II prototype, L4250, completed its maiden flight from Brooklands. The Merlins were over 100hp apiece, more powerful than the Pegasus engines, but, being water-cooled, they were also much heavier (the Mk II weighed 4,500lbs more than the Mk IC). However, the Mk II could fly higher and faster, but at the price of a lower bomb load and shorter maximum range.

This did not stop the mark being the first Wellington to be converted to carry the Barnes Wallis-designed 4,000lb 'Blockbuster' bomb, following modifications to the bomb bay. Production aircraft also incorporated long-range fuel tanks and tropicalisation, which would see the aircraft's all-up weight increase to 33,000lb.

Service

The Wellington Mk II first entered service with 12 and 142 squadrons at Binbrook in November 1940, later joining 9, 38, 57, 99, 104, 148, 158, 214, 218, 305, 405 and 466 squadrons. The first delivery of the effective 4,000lb bomb was carried out by a Mk II over Emden on 1 April 1941, the weapon only having been approved by the Ministry of Aircraft Production (MAP) in March.

Production

Two prototypes, L4250 and T2545, plus 399 Mk IIs were built in two main batches of 199 (in the range W5352–W5611) and 200 (in the range Z8328–Z8662), all of which were under the same contract number, B.7144/40, and all built at Weybridge.

Technical data – Wellington Mk II	
ENGINE	Two 1,145hp Rolls-Royce Merlin Xs
WINGSPAN	86ft 2in
LENGTH	64ft 7in
HEIGHT	17ft 5in
WING AREA	840 sq ft
EMPTY WEIGHT	20,258lb
GROSS WEIGHT	33,000lb
MAX SPEED	254mph at 17,500ft
SERVICE CEILING	23,500ft

Wellington Mk II W5379 before it was delivered to 12 Squadron at Binbrook in November 1940. The bomber crashed near Haamstede in the Netherlands during a raid on Cologne, 11 October 1941.

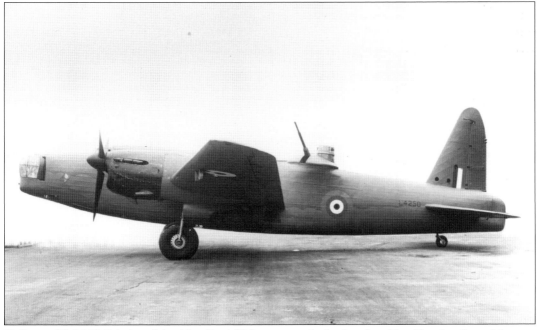

Wellington Mk II L4250 during trials with a 40mm Vickers cannon in the dorsal position. The aircraft was later modified with a twin-fin tail configuration.

Wellington Mk III

Development
The Wellington Mk III followed a similar path in its development, also being designed with an alternative powerplant; this time the Bristol Hercules. Orders to proceed with the Mk II and Mk III were issued simultaneously, with the intention of converting the tenth and 11th airframes from the initial production, but because of delays with both engines, the 38th and 39th were eventually selected.

Design
The first of two Mk III prototypes, L4251, was flown with Hercules HEISM engines on 19 May 1939, with Mutt Summers at the controls, R. C. Handasyde as flight test observer and Wg Cdr Rider-Young as the sole crewmember. The HEISM was a twin-stage supercharged engine, which was fitted with a 12ft 6in-diameter de Havilland constant-speed propeller.

Early flight trials proved disappointing, the expected superior performance over the Mk I was lacking, so the aircraft was sent to Bristol's for further development work. A second aircraft, ex-Mk IC P9238, was also converted to Mk III standard with Hercules III engines. Fitted with a Rotol electric propeller, this aircraft, after its maiden flight in January 1941, performed much more to expectations and was selected as the first production Mk III. This mark introduced a new rear FN20 turret with a much more effective quartet of .303in machine guns and de-icing equipment. Like the Mk II, the Mk III came straight from the production line with tropical equipment, including long-range fuel tanks and air filters over the engine intakes, making the type ideal for quickly re-equipping squadrons in the Middle East.

Service
The Mk III did not enter Bomber Command service until June 1941, but it would prove to be the mainstay until the re-equipment with the four-engined heavies began to gain momentum. The Mk III served with 9, 12, 37, 40, 57, 70, 75, 99, 101, 115, 142, 150, 156, 162, 166, 192, 196, 199, 300, 419, 420, 424, 425, 426, 427, 428 and 429 squadrons and was not withdrawn from Bomber Command frontline service until October 1943. However, it served with the OTUs until the end of the war.

Production
A total of 1,519 Mk IIIs were built; 780 of them at Blackpool, 737 at Chester and the two prototypes, L4251 and P9238, at Weybridge.

Technical data – Wellington Mk III	
ENGINE	Two 1,590hp Bristol Hercules HEISMs
WINGSPAN	86ft 2in
LENGTH	64ft 7in
HEIGHT	17ft 5in
WING AREA	840 sq ft
EMPTY WEIGHT	18,000lb
GROSS WEIGHT	28,500lb
MAX SPEED	255mph at 15,000ft
SERVICE CEILING	18,000ft
RANGE	2,200 miles with 1,500lb bomb load and 1,540 miles with 4,500lb bomb load

The prototype Mk III, L4251, which was actually the 39th production Mk I, at Boscombe Down during trials with the A&AEE.

The men and women who famously built the 'Broughton Bomber' (Mk III LN514) in 23 hours 50 minutes in the summer of 1943. The aircraft went on to serve with 19 OTU at Kinloss until it was SOC on 11 March 1943. (*Aeroplane*)

Warwick (B.1/95), B Mk I and B Mk II

Development

The Warwick started out as a heavy bomber version of the Wellington, an aircraft it shared a great deal with, including the geodetic airframe. Unfortunately, the Warwick as a bomber would prove unsuccessful because, from the outset, the Vickers' designers were forced into using an engine that would not achieve the modest performance figures demanded of the specification.

Design

Designed to specification B.1/35, the Vickers Type 284 was tendered to meet an Air Ministry requirement for a heavy bomber capable of carrying 2,000lb of bombs over a distant of 2,000 miles, with a cruising speed of no less than 195mph at 15,000ft. Another demand was that the wingspan should not be greater than 100ft, so that it could be easily moved in and out of the standard RAF hangars of the day.

The Vickers tender stated that the aircraft would be powered by the Bristol Hercules, which would have exceeded the above figures. However, as time rolled by, the bid by Vickers was compared to the later P.13/36 for which the Avro Manchester had been tendered, resulting in the Warwick prototype being fitted with the underdeveloped Rolls-Royce Vulture or Napier Sabre. As a result, two prototypes were ordered under the original B.1/35, modified to include one aircraft powered by the Vulture and the other the Napier.

Service

The first Vulture-powered Warwick prototype, serialled K8178, was initially flown by Mutt Summers out of Brooklands on 13 August 1939. However, the Rolls-Royce engine was already suffering from a variety of problems and as a result a number of restrictions were placed on it, making K8178 virtually useless from a developmental point of view. Attention then turned towards the second prototype, L9704, which by now was engine-less as all Napier engine production had been diverted solely to the Hawker Typhoon.

This gave Vickers the opportunity to fit the engine they really wanted, the Bristol Centaurus 18-cylinder sleeve-valve radial, and, with this powerplant, L9704 first flew on 5 April 1940. By now though, everything was focussed on producing the four-engine heavies, which led Vickers to look at another alternative engine for the Warwick. L9704 was then fitted with a pair of Pratt & Whitney Double Wasp R-2800-S1C4G engines, with which the aircraft first flew in July 1941.

With these powerplants a substantial production order was finally placed for the Warwick, the B Mk I with Wasp engines and the B Mk II with the Centaurus. However, the plan came to nothing when the expected delivery of 400 Wasp engines from the USA ended up being just 80. The Air Ministry contracts fell apart, and only 16 production B Mk Is were built, none of them ever entering operational service.

Production

Two B.1/95 prototypes, K8178 and L9704, and one B Mk II prototype, BV216, were built, followed by 16 production aircraft serialled BV214, BV215, BV217–BV222, BV228–BV230, BV291, BV293 and BV295–BV296. The original order, for 150 B Mk I and 100 B Mk IIs, was placed on 28 December 1940.

Technical data – Warwick Prototypes, B Mk I & II	
ENGINE	(P1) Two Rolls-Royce Vulture Is; (I) Two 1,850hp Pratt & Whitney Wasp R-2800-S1A4-Gs; (II) Two 2,000hp Bristol Centaurus IVs
WINGSPAN	96ft 8.5in
LENGTH	70ft
HEIGHT	18ft 6in
WING AREA	1,019 sq ft
GROSS WEIGHT	45,000lb
MAX SPEED	300mph at 20,000ft
SERVICE CEILING	28,200ft
RANGE	2,075 miles at 185mph at 15,000ft

Above: This is the first of two prototype Warwicks designed to B.1/35 and fitted with a pair of Rolls-Royce 24-cylinder X-type engines, which were later named Vultures. The under-developed engine was completely inadequate for the bomber, just as it had been for the Avro Manchester.

Right: The first production Warwick B Mk I, BV214, one of just 16 built, was first flown in April 1942. The aircraft was delivered to the A&AEE for trials but crashed on 26 August 1942, when a large section of wing fabric was lost.

Wellington Mk V and VI

Development

In 1938, a request was made to Vickers enquiring whether it was feasible to convert a Wellington to operate at altitudes between 35,000ft and 40,000ft, by using a pressurised cabin for the crew. Only Shorts and Fairey had experimented with pressure cabins before, specifically for civilian projects, which meant that Vickers would work from a blank sheet of paper. Despite no large orders materialising, the project was successful, and other manufacturers' aircraft would, in the future, benefit from Vickers' findings.

Design

The high-altitude Wellington was built in two versions, the Mk V (converted from Mk ICs) powered by Hercules engines and the Mk VI powered by Merlin 60 engines. The main feature of both aircraft was the remodelled forward fuselage containing the pressurised cabin, which was attached to the geodetic airframe by integral feet that were anchored to various nodal points. The pilot flew the aircraft from the upper section of the cabin through a small bubble canopy.

Designed to specifications B.23/29 and 17/40, the first Mk V, R3298, was fitted with a pair of Hercules III engines, while the second aircraft, R3299, had a pair of more powerful Hercules VIIIs, with exhaust-driven superchargers. However, the required ceiling was never reached, and attention turned to the Merlin-powered Mk VI instead.

Developed simultaneously with the Mk V, the Mk VI was powered by a pair of 1,600hp Rolls-Royce Merlin 60 engines fitted with a two-speed, two-stage supercharger designed for high-altitude flying. The Mk VI was produced fully equipped for high-altitude bombing, and provision was made for a pilot, navigator, bomb-aimer and wireless operator within the pressurised cabin. Armament was planned to be a pressurised Fraser-Nash FN70 rear turret, mounting four .303in machine guns, but an FN20A was fitted at first because the FN70 was still under development.

Service

The first of just three Mk V prototypes, R3298, was initially flown from Brooklands on 25 September 1940 direct to Blackpool, following the Luftwaffe attack that hit the Weybridge factory earlier in the month. Flight trials began on 21 October, with a climb to 20,000ft, which had to be curtailed as the pilot's canopy iced up. Further flights continued until 30,000ft was reached on 31 October, which was as high as any Mk V could climb, simply because the Hercules engines were out of their optimum performance zone.

The Mk VI was more successful. The first of 64 built, W5795, first flew in November 1941. The Merlin 60 engines were more suited to high-altitude work, and the Mk VI was capable of reaching 40,000ft, as was required by the Air Ministry.

It was hoped that the Mk VI could serve as a specialised pathfinder aircraft for Bomber Command, and four aircraft did serve with 109 Squadron at Tempsford and Stradishall between March and July 1942. However, the only readily available and suitable aircraft for this task was the Mosquito, which 109 Squadron converted to in December 1942.

Production

Three Mk Vs, serialled R3298, R3299 and W5796, and 64 Mk VIs serialled W5795, W5796–W5815, DR471–DR504, DR519–DR528 (DR485–DR527 were Mk VIAs) were built.

Technical data – Wellington Mk V & VI	
ENGINE	(V) Two Bristol Hercules VIIIs; (VI) Two Rolls-Royce Merlin 60s
WINGSPAN	86ft 2in
LENGTH	(V) 64ft 7in; (VI) 61ft 9in
HEIGHT	17ft 5in
WING AREA	840 sq ft
SERVICE CEILING	(V) 30,000ft; (VI) 40,000ft
RANGE	(VI) 1,590 miles with 4,500lb bomb load and 2,275 miles with 1,500lb load

Above: The prototype Wellington Mk V, R3298, which was flown north, away from the attentions of the Luftwaffe, in September 1940. The aircraft, fitted with Hercules engines, could not quite reach the criteria laid down by the Air Ministry.

Below left: DR484 was one of four aircraft that served with 109 Squadron at Tempsford and Stradishall between March and July 1942. The aircraft was also trialled by the A&AEE until it was SOC on 30 December 1943.

Below right: A view from the access door of the pressurised cabin of a Mk V, showing the wireless operator's position on the left-hand side. The cabin was mounted so that it could expand and contract independently of the geodetic structure.

Wellington Mk IV

Development

By the beginning of World War Two, the rate at which Wellington airframes were being produced was exceeding engine production by a considerable margin. The amount of liquid-cooled Merlin engines available was also reducing, as these were being diverted to fighter production. The only option was to look overseas, and while the US aircraft industry was the first choice, Alfa Romeo was also considered, because at this stage of the war, Italy was neutral.

Design

On 9 September 1939, a contract was placed with the American manufacturer Pratt & Whitney for a pair of their Twin Wasp SC3-9 engines to be fitted to a single prototype. By February 1940, the US government had given permission for the more powerful R-2800 to be made available to the British. This was a heavier engine, but it was equal in power to the planned Hercules-powered version of the Wellington. After Rex Pierson made a request to the Air Ministry for the R-2800, the reply was that a decision had been made to cancel the Wasp engine in favour of the Wright Cyclone GR-1820/C2054, but this option was also later cancelled.

After this period of indecision, the apparent imminent invasion of Britain by July 1940 saw the option of American engines examined again. On 27 July, a decision was finally made to install the 1,050hp Twin Wasp R-183S3C4-C engine into the Wellington, which would become the Mk IV. All other systems of the Mk IV were little different from the Mk IC and performance figures compared to the Mk III.

Service

Just four months after instructions to proceed were received from the Air Ministry, the first Twin Wasp-powered Mk IV, R1220, undertook its maiden flight from Hawarden in the hands of Maurice Hare in December 1940. All Mk IV production would subsequently be carried out at Chester, and the first of 220 aircraft built began entering service from August 1941. The Wellington Mk IV served with 142, 300, 301, 305, 458, 460 and 544 squadrons before it was phased out from Bomber Command's frontline operations by March 1943.

Production

In total, 220 Mk IVs were all built at Hawarden, including the prototype, ex-Mk IC R1220, plus 24 others drawn from the same Mk IC batch. The main contract for 195 new-build Mk IVs was placed at Hawarden to contract B97887/40 in the serial ranges Z1182–Z1183, Z1202–Z1292, Z1311–Z1345 and Z1375–Z1496. This entire batch was delivered between June 1941 and March 1942.

Technical data – Wellington Mk IV	
ENGINE	Two 1,050hp Twin Wasp R-183S3C4-Cs
WINGSPAN	86ft 2in
LENGTH	64ft 7in
HEIGHT	17ft 5in
WING AREA	840 sq ft
GROSS WEIGHT	31,500lb
MAX SPEED	255mph at 15,000ft
SERVICE CEILING	18,000ft
RANGE	1,500 miles

The prototype Mk IV, R1220, was drawn from the Mk IC production along with the next 24 aircraft built. After its maiden flight in December 1940, the aircraft suffered from vibration problems, which were cured by fitting a pair of Curtiss electric propellers.

Wellington Mk X

Development

By the time the development of the Wellington had reached the Mk III stage, the aircraft had reached its maximum loading. Further improvement of the type seemed unlikely, until a new light alloy was produced with a much higher load capacity. When the new alloy was made available to Vickers, the Wellington was given a new lease of life.

Design

Incorporating the new alloy into the structure of the Wellington caused very few problems, and it enabled the aircraft to have a much greater all-up weight without increasing the weight of the airframe itself. The opportunity was also taken to install the high-powered 1,675hp Bristol Hercules VI or XVI engines.

To test the new engines, a Mk III, X3374, was drawn from the Blackpool production line and trialled as the Mk X prototype, powered by a pair of Hercules VI engines. By July 1942, the first production Type 440 Mk X, DF609, left the Blackpool production line, a few weeks behind schedule. All Mk X production was subsequently shared between Blackpool and Chester, HE147 being the first built at the latter.

Service

The Mk X was destined to have a short career in the front line with Bomber Command; the type arriving in December 1942 with 431 Squadron at Burn. It had, however, been withdrawn from Bomber Command by October 1943 in favour of the four-engine heavies. The Mk X quickly took over all of the roles of the Mk III; its improved performance and reliability being appreciated by the crews.

The Mk X remained in frontline service in the RAF, performing general duties in many theatres, and it was even retained in the bomber role in the Middle East, North Africa and India until the end of the war, serving with 28 operational squadrons. These were 36, 37, 40, 70, 99, 104, 142, 150, 162, 166, 192, 196, 199, 215, 300, 304, 305, 420, 424, 425, 426, 427, 428, 429, 431, 432, 466 and 527 squadrons.

In the second line, the abundance of Mk Xs resulted in the hard-pressed bomber OTUs being re-equipped with the type, many of them retaining the aircraft into the immediate post-war period. Many Mk Xs were converted into trainers, and the type also proved most adaptable as an engine testbed, including one aircraft, LN715, which carried out sterling work in the development of the Rolls-Royce Dart turboprop.

Production

In total, 3,803 Mk Xs were built at Blackpool and Chester from 1942 to 25 October 1945, when the last aircraft, RP590, was delivered to the RAF from Blackpool.

Technical data – Wellington Mk X	
ENGINE	Two 1,675hp Hercules VI/XVIs
WINGSPAN	86ft 2in
LENGTH	64ft 7in
HEIGHT	17ft 6in
WING AREA	840 sq ft
EMPTY WEIGHT	22,474lb
GROSS WEIGHT	36,500lb
MAX SPEED	255mph
SERVICE CEILING	22,000ft
RANGE	1,885 miles at 180mph with 1,500lb bomb load

The Mk X represented the pinnacle of development for the Wellington in the bomber role, but from this mark would spring a host of other Coastal Command and trainer variants. Blackpool-built HZ470, having served previously with 424 and 429 squadrons and 83 OTU, undertakes a training sortie during its final tour of RAF duty with 86 OTU at Gamston.

Type 432 (F.7/41)

Development

The roots of the Type 432 were first laid in 1939, when there was a requirement for a new twin-engined fighter to be fitted with 20mm or 40mm cannon. The aircraft would eventually be designed to a requirement for a high-flying fighter capable of intercepting Junkers bombers, which appeared early in the war and were expected to attack Britain in large numbers. As the war progressed, these attacks never materialised, but the same specification F.7/41, which the Type 432 was finally built to, did see the Westland Welkin enter limited production, although none of the 60 built ever went into service.

Design

The Type 432 bore a passing resemblance to the de Havilland Mosquito. The twin-engined monoplane was the first Vickers aircraft to be of stressed-skin construction. The fuselage looked like a streamlined tube, which had a flush-fitting skin that was attached to spaced circular frames. The entire airframe was flush-riveted in an effort to reduce drag. The wing was a very novel design known as a 'lobster claw', the structure being made from a heavy gauge skin, which had a thicker section to fit a pair of span-wise spar booms at the centre top and bottom of the aerofoil.

Service

The aircraft was built inside the secret prototype hangar located at Foxwarren, halfway between Weybridge and Wisley. The complete aircraft, serialled DZ217, was taken by road to Farnborough for taxi trials and its maiden flight. The taxi trials were not straightforward, and test pilot Tommy Lucke struggled to get the aircraft to run in a straight line. This was cured by moving the position of the undercarriage 3in to the rear.

On 24 December 1942, Lucke flew DZ217 for the first time, but all was not well. The aircraft refused to make a three-point landing, caused by the tailplane stalling near the ground and an overbalance of the ailerons. This was cured with various adjustments and a set of Irving-type ailerons.

Performance wise, the Type 432 fell below expectations, with the aircraft's Merlin 61 engines refusing to run properly above 23,000ft. The Type 432 was only flown 28 times, 25 of these were by Tommy Lucke. The best performance achieved by the aircraft was on 14 May 1943, when 380mph was reached at 15,000ft, but this was still way below the expected 435mph at 28,000ft the aircraft was designed for.

A second aircraft was cancelled on 1 May 1943, and by the end of the year the entire programme was scrubbed. DZ217 was kept by Vickers in an airworthy state until the end of 1944 in support of the B.3/42 Windsor project, but is believed to have been scrapped by early 1945.

Technical data – F.7/41	
ENGINE	Two 1,520hp Rolls-Royce Merlin 61s
WINGSPAN	56ft 10½in
LENGTH	39ft 3in
HEIGHT	13ft 9in
WING AREA	450 sq ft
EMPTY WEIGHT	16,373lb
LOADED WEIGHT	54,000lb
MAX SPEED	380mph at 15,000ft
CLIMB RATE	2,750ft/min
SERVICE CEILING	38,500ft
RANGE	1,500 miles

Right: Vickers test pilot, Tommy Lucke, is at the controls of the only Type 432 (F.7/41) built, DZ217, during one of his 25 experimental flights in the aircraft. (*Aeroplane*)

Below: The Type 432 at the rear of the Foxwarren complex, which was located between Brooklands and Wisley, south of the junction of the Byfleet and Redhill roads. Until 2011, one original building remained; however, the site is now covered with modern housing. (*Aeroplane*)

Wellington GR Mk XI, XII, XIII and XIV

Development

The outstanding design of the Mk X airframe also provided the basis for many variants of the Wellington family, including the GR (General Reconnaissance) types that served Coastal Command from late 1942 to the end of the war.

Design

The first of the four variants using the Mk X airframe was GR Mk XI, which was similar to its older sibling, only differing by having a Type 454 ASW Mk II radar fitted, a retractable Leigh light under the rear fuselage and the provision to carry a pair of 18in torpedoes. Introduced in January 1943, the Mk XI joined the Mk XII, which had entered service one month earlier. The main difference with the Mk XII was the ASV Mk III radar, which was contained within a teardrop fairing under the chin of the bomber, while the previous system relied on numerous external aerials. The new radar equipment forced the removal of the front turret, which initially made the aircraft vulnerable to attack from any U-boat that was prepared to fight it out on the surface. A pair of Browning machine guns, on flexible mounts, were later installed in the Mk XIIs.

The GR Mk XIII and the GR Mk XIV were both fitted with 1,735hp Hercules XVII engines and Leigh lights. The Mk XIII served as a torpedo bomber with ASV Mk II radar, while the Mk XIV, fitted with ASV Mk III radar, fulfilled an anti-submarine role; some were operated with RPs on rails mounted outboard of the engines and depth charges.

Service

The GR Mk XI was the second of the Mk X GR derivatives to enter service when it was delivered to 407 Squadron at Docking in January 1943. While the type's service with 407 Squadron was short, six other units were equipped with the mark, and the last, 344 Squadron at Dakar, did not retire its aircraft until November 1945.

The GR Mk XII was the first of the new generation of Coastal Command Wellingtons to enter service, when it joined 172 Squadron at Chivenor in December 1942. The type did not enjoy a long service career and was withdrawn by February 1944. The GR Mk XIII was the most used of the three variants, serving with 17 Coastal Command squadrons from July 1943 right through to April 1946, when the type was retired by 294 Squadron at Idku.

The final variant, the GR Mk XIV, served with 11 RAF squadrons from June 1943 to December 1946. The type was first issued to an auxiliary unit, 612 (County of Aberdeen) Squadron at Chivenor and was retired by 38 Squadron at Grottaglie.

The maritime type Wellingtons were used extensively by Coastal Command as well as overseas. Their contribution was outstanding, and their involvement in the war against the U-boats resulted in them sinking 26 enemy submarines and damaging many more.

Production

In total, 180 GR Mk XIs, 58 GR Mk XIIs, 844 GR Mk XIIIs and GR Mk 841 XIVs were built between 1943 and 1945.

Technical data – Wellington Mk XI, XII, XVII & XIV	
ENGINE	(XI & XII) Two 1,675hp Hercules VI/XVIs; (XVII & XIV) Two 1,735hp Hercules XVIIs
WINGSPAN	86ft 2in
LENGTH	64ft 7in
HEIGHT	17ft 5in
WING AREA	840 sq ft
EMPTY WEIGHT	22,474lb
GROSS WEIGHT	36,500lb
MAX SPEED	255mph
SERVICE CEILING	22,000ft
RANGE	1,885 miles at 180mph with 1,500lb bomb load

GR MK XIV MP714 during RP (Rocket Projectile) trials with the A&AEE in 1943. The aircraft later served with 612 and 179 squadrons and finally 6 OTU at Kinloss, and it was not SOC until 27 March 1943.

The ASW Mk II equipped GR Mk XI served the RAF from January 1943 until November 1945. MP521 was delivered to 407 Squadron, but it was later one of many ex-Coastal Command Wellingtons that were transferred to the Federal Aviation Administration (FAA). The type served with five second-line FAA units; 716, 736, 758, 762 and 765 squadrons.

Warwick C Mk I and C Mk III

Development

Following the failure of the Warwick as a bomber, it was recognised from an early stage that the aircraft would be suited to the more passive role of troop transport and general duties. However, the idea lay dormant until 1942 when an order for 14 Warwicks was received from BOAC.

Design

The plan was to have delivered the entire order to BOAC by the end of 1942, but this was to prove optimistic. A great deal of modification work was needed to convert the B Mk I into a C Mk I, including the removal of all military equipment and the installation of cabin windows, a strengthened freight floor, exhaust flame dampers and very-long-range fuel tanks. The first aircraft, BV243, was initially flown on 5 February 1943.

The development of the C Mk I and the C MK III mainly differed by the latter having a large ventral freight-pannier added in place of the bomb bay doors. These contained four 125-gallon fuel tanks.

Service

The Warwick C Mk I first joined BOAC in 1943, the type being employed to fly mail, freight and passengers of the British forces serving in North Africa at the time. Their service with the civilian airline was short, and by late 1944 all had been transferred to RAF Transport Command to serve with 167 Squadron based at Holmsley South.

Then Warwick C Mk III first joined 46 and 47 Group, RAF Transport Command, which operated the type across the Mediterranean theatre, Italy and Greece from early 1945 to March 1946. The general serviceability rate of the Warwick was poor in RAF service, the aircraft seemingly unable to cope with high temperatures, which ruled it out of any Far Eastern service.

The aircraft performed better on routes between the United Kingdom and the Middle East, and in this capacity the type joined 525 Squadron, operating out of Lyneham in June 1944, followed by 167 Squadron at Blackbushe in November. The same month the type was issued to 353 Squadron at Palem in India, but the Warwick's fabric covering did not stand up well to the tropical conditions and the aircraft was withdrawn in June 1945.

In the UK, two Polish units, 301 Squadron at Blackbushe and 304 Squadron at North Weald, both of whom had been operating ex-BOAC C Mk Is, received the C Mk III in May and July 1945, respectively. 304 Squadron became the last unit to operate the Warwick when it replaced it with the Halifax C Mk VIII at Chedburgh in May 1946.

Production

Fourteen Warwick B Mk 1s were converted to C Mk 1 standard, initially serialled BV243–BV256, but re-registered as G-AGEX to G-AGFK in BOAC service. In total, 100 Warwick C Mk IIIs were built for the RAF, serialled HG215–HG256, HG271–HG307 and HG320–HG340.

Technical data – Warwick C Mk III	
ENGINE	Two 1,850hp Pratt & Whitney Double Wasp R-2800-S1A4-Gs
WINGSPAN	96ft 8½in
LENGTH	70ft 6in
HEIGHT	18ft 6in
WING AREA	1,006 sq ft
EMPTY WEIGHT	29,162lb
GROSS WEIGHT	46,000lb
MAX SPEED	260mph at 5,000ft
CLIMB RATE	675 ft/min
SERVICE CEILING	15,000ft
RANGE	2,150 miles at 180mph at 15,000ft with 24 troops or 6,170lb load

Right: The last of 14 Warwick C Mk Is delivered to the British Overseas Airways Corporation (BOAC) in 1943 was ex-BV256, re-registered as G-AGFK. The aircraft was later transferred to 525 Squadron at Weston Zoyland and was not SOC until 29 July 1947. (Charles E. Brown)

Below: The most obvious difference between the C Mk I and the C Mk III is clearly shown in this view of HG215. The large pannier along the lower fuselage contained four 125-gallon fuel tanks. HG215 was the first C Mk III built for the RAF, however, the aircraft never entered operational service and was only recorded as being on the strength of the A&AEE.

Wellington T Mk XVII, XVIII, X and XIX

Development

The dedicated purpose-built Wellington trainer was a long time coming, as the early marks were already fitted with dual controls, which made pilot training a lot easier. These were coupled to the main controls and were mounted on a floor extension, positioned forward of the starboard seat.

As specialist training OTUs began to form in numbers during the early stages of the war, many ex-operational Wellingtons were handed down to these units, and many more were converted with dual controls. As more specialist training was required and the number of surplus Wellingtons began to increase, the type found itself being converted into navigation, radio operator and airborne interception (AI) training aircraft.

Design

In numerical order, the T Mk XVII was the first of the main trainer variants, which were converted from ex-Hercules XVII-powered GR Mk XI Coastal Command Wellingtons. The aircraft was modified to train night-fighter crews, and the nose turret was replaced by a Mosquito-type SCR 720 AI radar set. The rear turret was also removed from this first purpose-built Wellington 'flying classroom'.

The next Wellington trainer was the T Mk XVIII, which was a conversion of the B Mk X and GR Mk XIII and was also employed to train radar operators. Equipped as per the T Mk XVII, the aircraft had room for four pupils and an instructor. All of the conversion work for this mark was carried out at Blackpool where new-build aircraft were also produced.

A large number of B Mk Xs were converted by Boulton Paul at Wolverhampton into dual-control T Mk Xs during the post-war period. The airframes were completely stripped, overhauled and recovered and then fully fitted out as navigation trainers. Once again, both the nose and rear turrets were removed and faired over.

The final variant was the T Mk XIX (T.19), which was converted 'in-house' by the RAF in 1946 from several surplus Wellington B Mk Xs. The aircraft was used as a basic multi-engine trainer prior to the arrival of the Valetta and Varsity.

Service

As a dual-controlled aircraft, the Wellington was able to serve as its own 'trainer' when it first entered service. The dedicated variants began seeing service from 1943 onwards, while the T Mk X and T Mk XIX were introduced to training units from 1946. The T Mk X was destined to be the last Wellington in RAF service when it was retired by the Air Navigation School in March 1953, to be replaced by the Valetta T Mk 3. Several T Mk Xs were also sold to France and Greece.

Production

Nine T Mk XVIIs were converted from GR Mk XIs, 80 T Mk XVIIIs were converted at Blackpool from GR Mk XIIIs, and 270 ex-B Mk Xs were converted to T Mk X (T.10) trainers by Boulton Paul between January 1946 and 20 March 1952. An unknown number of B Mk X airframes were converted by the RAF to T Mk XIX standard.

Technical data – Wellington T Mk X	
ENGINE	Two 1,675hp Hercules VI/XVIs
WINGSPAN	86ft 2in
LENGTH	64ft 7in
HEIGHT	17ft 6in
WING AREA	840 sq ft
EMPTY WEIGHT	22,474lb
GROSS WEIGHT	36,500lb
MAX SPEED	255mph
SERVICE CEILING	22,000ft
RANGE	2,000 miles

Originally built as a GR Mk XI, the first tour of duty for MP530 was with 407 Squadron before the bomber was converted into a T Mk XVII trainer. Along with several others, it was initially transferred to the FAA, but gave little service before it was returned to the RAF to serve with 51 and 54 OTUs until May 1947.

By far the most prolifically produced of the Wellington trainers, the T Mk X was also the last example of the type to see RAF service, retiring in March 1953. RP589 is pictured at Brooklands in January 1949.

Wellington C Mk IX, XV and XVI

Development
From the outset, the concept of utilising the Wellington as a civilian or military transport was considered, but despite several proposals being put forward before the outbreak of World War Two, none came to fruition. Several Wellington Mk Is were converted 'ad hoc' as passenger-carrying aircraft, usually for bespoke specialist operations, rather than as a production run. However, in 1941, the Air Ministry asked Vickers to begin preparing technical information for a freight and/or troop-carrying variant of the Wellington. At the same time, a high-priority request was issued by the RAF's Middle East Command for transport aircraft to increase the mobility of forces in the region.

Design
The request, at first, involved a basic conversion of the Wellington bomber to transport troops and their equipment by removing all unnecessary military paraphernalia. This included the space-consuming oxygen equipment to make way for seats, which were of a similar pattern to those fitted into the pre-war Valentia.

Aircraft converted were ex-Mk ICs, IIs, IIIs and IVs, and the transformation from bomber to transport aircraft was not just carried out at Weybridge, but also at RAF stations across the globe; as a result, the number of Wellingtons that were changed to this more passive role is unknown.

As demand grew for transport aircraft, Vickers began converting much larger numbers, especially as more ex-Bomber Command Mk I, IA and IC variants became available. At least 100 Mk ICs were converted, which finally justified the type having a proper designation, and from 1943 the aircraft were referred to as the C Mk IA and C Mk IC. However, this designation, which would become more familiar to transport aircraft during the post-war years, was dropped in favour of the C Mk XV and C Mk XVI, respectively.

The Type 437 Wellington Mk IX was indicative of the entire series of transport aircraft and could carry 18 fully equipped troops with a range of between 1,000 and 2,000 miles, depending on the load being carried.

Service
Little is recorded regarding which aircraft served with particular units, and only the brief service of the C Mk XVI is known. This mark first joined 24 Squadron at Hendon in February 1943, but it was retired by January 1944. The type did not reappear in the records until 232 and 242 squadrons were re-formed at Stoney Cross, in the heart of the New Forest, on 15 November 1944. 232 Squadron received its first aircraft in December 1944, but had retired them in favour of the Liberator Mk VII by February 1945, while 242 Squadron received its first C Mk XVI in January 1945, but only kept them a few weeks before they were replaced by the much larger Stirling Mk V.

Technical data – Wellington C Mk IX, XV & XVI	
ENGINE	(XVI) Two 1,050hp Bristol Pegasus XVIIIs
WINGSPAN	86ft 2in
LENGTH	64ft 7in
HEIGHT	17ft 5in
WING AREA	840 sq ft
MAX SPEED	235mph at 10,000ft
RANGE	(IX) 1,000 to 2,000 miles

Having already served with the New Zealand Flight (as NZ502), and 15 and 27 OTUs, this ex-Wellington Mk I was converted to a C Mk I, reverting to its original production serial, L4340, and serving with 24 Squadron at Hendon. Named the *Duke of Rutland*, the aircraft served until November 1944.

The C Mk XVI, originally designated the C Mk IC, was a transport conversion of the Mk IC bomber variant. Wellington C Mk XVI, N2875, was not officially allocated to a transport unit, and instead the aircraft saw out its days with the Central Gunnery School and was SOC in January 1946.

Warwick ASR Mk I and Mk VI

Development

By early 1943, the Air Staff made it clear that the Warwick did not have a future as a bomber, but it could be useful in the air-sea rescue (ASR) role and as a freighter. With regard to the ASR role, the aircraft would have to be modified to carry Lindholme gear (five cylindrical containers, one with a nine-man dinghy and the rest with survival equipment) or an airborne lifeboat. By May 1943, an order for 100 Warwick ASRs had been placed.

Design

The requirements for the Warwick ASR Mk I were simple: the aircraft must be able to carry two sets of Lindholme gear and/or a Mk I lifeboat, and be able to drop it at a speed between 100–130mph. The aircraft needed to carry a crew of seven without oxygen equipment, and with the lifeboat attached a specified range of 1,800 miles needed to be achieved.

None of this was a problem for the Warwick; it was now a case of producing a bespoke lifeboat. Designed by Uffa Fox, CBE, an English boat maker, the Mk I lifeboat was fitted with engines and rocket gear plus survival equipment, but still only weighed about 1,630lb. Before live trials, a 1/13 scale model was tested in an RAE wind tunnel, while a lifeboat was first dropped by a Hudson, off Cowes, with good results.

The first production version of the Warwick ASR was referred to as the Stage A, which was designed to carry, as originally specified, a lifeboat and two sets of Lindholme gear. Nine aircraft, beginning with BV298, were converted to this standard and trialled at Boscombe Down. Three Stage As were first to enter RAF service.

The Stage B, of which 20 were built, which could also be fitted with an ASV radar in the wing, had aerials mounted along the front fuselage and an FN24 rear turret fitted. The finalised version of the Warwick ASR, the Stage C, was redesignated as the ASR Mk I and encompassed both the A and B specification. This mark could operate in four different layouts, firstly with a Mk I lifeboat at 42,924lb, Lindholme gear only at 41,534lb, a Mk II Lifeboat at 44,764lb and with extra fuel tanks with a potential range of 2,000 miles at 41,984lb.

Service

The Warwick ASR Mk I entered service with 280 Squadron at Thornaby in October 1943, although three Stage As had already arrived in August while the unit was at Bircham Newton. The ASR Mk I went on to serve with 38, 251, 269, 276, 277, 278, 279, 280, 281, 282, 283, 284, 292, 293 and 294 squadrons, of which seven of these units were based in the United Kingdom and the remainder were stationed overseas.

The first successful Mk IA lifeboat rescue by a Warwick took place on 9 January 1944, when it was dropped for a Mosquito crew off Land's End. Another example was when a lifeboat was dropped to another Mosquito crew in the southern part of the Bay of Biscay; incredibly, after four days at sea the duo made it back home.

Production

Nine Stage As were built, plus 20 Stage Bs followed by 204 of the main production variant, the ASR Mk I; serials ranged from BV223–HG214. In total, 94 Mk VIs, powered by Double Wasp R-2800-2SBG engines were built, although only two entered RAF service.

Technical data – Warwick ASR Mk I	
ENGINE	Two 1,850hp Pratt & Whitney Double Wasp R-2800-S1A4-Gs
WINGSPAN	96ft 8½in
LENGTH	70ft 6in
HEIGHT	18ft 6in
WING AREA	1,006 sq ft
EMPTY WEIGHT	28,154lb
GROSS WEIGHT	45,000lb
MAX SPEED	224mph at 3,600ft
CLIMB RATE	660 ft/min
SERVICE CEILING	21,500ft
RANGE	2,300 miles at 150mph at 5,000ft

Right: A 269 Squadron Warwick ASR Mk I had its Uffa Fox-designed Lifeboat Mk I positioned under the fuselage. The unit operated the type from Lagens in the Azores from September 1944 through to March 1946.

Below left: 282 Squadron was reformed with the Warwick ASR Mk I at Davidstow Moor on 1 February 1944. HF944 was serving at the time of the D-Day landings in June 1944 and remained with the unit until July 1946.

Below right: Reformed from 1407 Flight on 1 August 1944, 251 Squadron operated in the ASR role from Reykjavik, Iceland, until October 1945. One of the units ASR Mk Is is pictured during an open day in the summer of 1945.

Warwick GR Mk II, II Met and GR Mk V

Development

The Warwick Mk II was given a new lease of life in the GR role thanks to the increasing availability of the Bristol Centaurus engine. Two variants were planned as the main production types, one capable of carrying a pair of 18in or 24in torpedoes and the other a radar equipped variant complete with Leigh light.

Design

By May 1943, the Leigh light version of what was to be designated the GR Mk II was cancelled. Instead, the aircraft, which was powered by a pair of Centaurus CE7SM engines, had provision for 12–15 depth charges and a dozen RPs in the early production aircraft. Another descendent of the Warwick Mk II was the GR (Met) Mk II, which was used for meteorological duties and high-altitude navigation training. All bomb gear was removed from the 'Mets', the nose turret was replaced by a wide-vision nose window, and an oxygen system was also installed.

The GR Mk V was the most successful of this group of Warwicks and was the first Centaurus-powered variant to enter service. The first aircraft, PN697, completed its maiden flight in April 1944. The GR Mk V was similar to the GR Mk II, but it was fitted with a radar scanner under the nose and a Leigh light, installed at a fixed inclination of 7°, in the ventral position. The mid-upper turret was also removed and a pair of 0.5in Browning machine guns was fitted into the beam position instead. Initial directional instability problems were cured by a dorsal fin being fitted in front of the main fin.

Service

The GR Mk II never entered operational service, but it was allocated to 6 and 26 OTU and the Empire Air Navigation School, although the odd aircraft did briefly serve with 38 and 524 squadrons. The few GR (Met) Mk IIs built did not enter operational service, but the GR Mk V did, first joining 179 Squadron at St Eval in November 1944. 621 Squadron also operated the GR Mk V, from January 1945 at Mersah Matruh, Eygpt, but had the war lasted longer the aircraft would have been delivered to many more units.

Post-war, 32 GR Mk Vs also served with 17 and 27 squadrons, South African Air Force, from May 1945 to March 1946 and March to December 1945, respectively. The aircraft of 179 Squadron were retired in May 1946 and 621 Squadron's in August 1946. Both RAF units were re-equipped with Lancaster GR Mk IIIs.

Production

In total, 119 GR Mk IIs (HG341–HG512), 14 GR (Met) Mk IIs (HG513–HG525 and HG533–HG539) and 236 GR Mk Vs (ranging from LM777–PN682) were built, followed by an order for 116 GR Mk VIs, which was cancelled.

Technical data – Warwick GR Mk II	
ENGINE	Two 2,500hp Bristol Centaurus VIs
WINGSPAN	96ft 8½in
LENGTH	68ft 6in
HEIGHT	18ft 6in
WING AREA	1,006 sq ft
EMPTY WEIGHT	31,125lb
GROSS WEIGHT	51,250lb
MAX SPEED	262mph at 2,000ft
SERVICE CEILING	19,000ft
RANGE	3,050 miles at 161mph at 5,000ft

The second production Vickers Warwick GR Mk V, PN698, during trials with the A&AEE in 1944. This aircraft never joined an operational unit and was SOC on 20 August 1947.

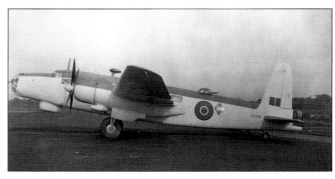

A good example of an early production Warwick GR Mk II is HG348, pictured here in November 1944. Although the type never saw operational service, HG348 was briefly on the strength of 524 Squadron, whose main equipment was the Wellington GR Mk XIV.

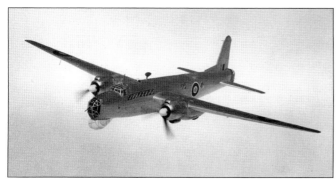

A product of the second batch of 109 GR Mk Vs built at Weybridge and delivered between May 1945 and April 1946, this aircraft, LM818, was one of a few that actually saw operational service, albeit in peacetime. The aircraft, complete with a clear Perspex ASV blister (which appears to be empty), served with 179 Squadron, 1 FU and the TFU before it was retired in May 1950.

Windsor

Development

It was third time lucky for Rex Pierson, who had already tried and failed to secure orders for bomber specifications B.12/36 and B.1/39, before two prototypes were requested in response to his tender for B.5/41. This was for a four-engined, high-altitude bomber with a pressurised cabin capable of operating at over 30,000ft and nearly 350mph. After a considerable amount of effort had been spent designing the pressurised cabin, the specification was changed to B.3/42, which deleted the need for the cabin and saw the design settle on the designation, Type 447, later named the Windsor.

Design

The design was heavily based on the Warwick, but used a high-aspect ratio wing, which was originally used in the B.12/36 tender. Geodetic construction was employed throughout the airframe and power was provided by four Merlin 60 two-stage, twin-supercharged, engines. The undercarriage was made up of four main units, each of them retracting into an engine nacelle. Armament was, at first, to be a conventional fore and aft turret arrangement, but, in February 1943, the Air Ministry requested that a pair of remotely controlled barbettes with four 20mm cannon apiece be fitted into the rear of the inboard engine nacelles. The firing of these weapons would be the responsibility of one fire-control crewman, who sighted, controlled and fired the guns using an automatic gun-laying radar system located in the tail of the bomber.

Service

The first Type 447 Windsor, serialled DW506, undertook its maiden flight from Farnborough on 23,October 1943, in the hands of Mutt Summers. Initial take-off weight was restricted to 46,000lb, and early performance figures were encouraging with 302mph at 25,000ft recorded. However, the aircraft's flying was destined to be short-lived, because on 2 March 1944, DW506 was damaged beyond repair in a forced landing and was broken up for component testing.

The second aircraft, DW512, designated as the Type 457, differed by having a set of Merlin 85 engines complete with annular cowlings. This aircraft first flew from Wisley on 15 February 1944. A third aircraft, NK136, designated as the Type 461, initially flew on 11 July 1944. Meanwhile, flight trials with DW512 had revealed that the wing fabric had an alarming tendency to balloon. The problem was partly cured by applying a heavyweight, wire-backed fabric, the wings of NK136 being used to trial it. As a result, the top speed of NK136 was reduced by 25mph because of the heavier fabric. Only NK136 was fitted with armament, after the barbettes were successfully trialled by Warwick L9704.

By 1943, the Air Ministry committed to an order for five prototypes and 300 production aircraft, but by the end of World War Two only three prototypes had been built. A fourth prototype, serialled NN670, which was intended to be the first production aircraft with Merlin 100 engines, was close to completion when the entire Windsor programme was cancelled in March 1946.

The production Windsor B Mk I was to have been fitted with Rolls-Royce Griffons, while a proposed B Mk II would have been powered by four 3,020shp Rolls-Royce Clyde axial-flow turboprops.

Technical data – Windsor	
ENGINE	Four 1,635hp Rolls-Royce Merlin 65s
WINGSPAN	117ft 2in
LENGTH	76ft 10in
HEIGHT	23ft
WING AREA	1,248 sq ft
EMPTY WEIGHT	38,606lb
LOADED WEIGHT	54,000lb
MAX SPEED	317mph at 23,000ft
CLIMB RATE	1,250ft/min
SERVICE CEILING	27,500ft
RANGE	2,890 miles with an 8,000lb bomb load

Above left: Although a total of five prototypes were ordered by 1943, only three ever flew, and a fourth was never completed. This is the third and final prototype Windsor, NK136, not long after its maiden flight in July 1944.

Above right: Mutt Summers taxies the first prototype, Type 447 Windsor DW506, at Farnborough, prior to its maiden flight on 23 October 1943.

A daring design from every angle, the Windsor was planned for use against the Japanese in the Pacific if the war had been drawn out any longer. However, it is doubtful whether the aircraft would have performed as well as Vickers claimed, because of the fragility of the fabric covering and the fact there was no provision for defence from a frontal fighter attack.

Viking Mk IA, IB and C Mk 2

Development

The Brabazon Committee, which was formed in late 1942 to discuss and prepare the future of the British commercial airliner, made no provision for the immediate post-war period, despite the fact that types conceived by the committee would not enter service until the early 1950s at best. Stop-gap types, such as the Vickers Commercial (VC), were not factored in, although the aircraft would serve airlines across the globe in healthy numbers into the 1960s.

The government did recognise that some 'interim' types were needed, however, and in October 1944, three prototypes were ordered to specification 17/44. By December, the designer Rex Pierson had presented the technical aspects of the VC.1 to the Brabazon Committee, which expressed a great deal of interest in the aircraft despite the airliner not fitting into any of the committee's requirements.

Design

The Type 491 Viking had an immediate advantage from the start, because it made full use of the many tried and tested Wellington and Warwick components. The pace of development was accelerated as the early examples made use of the Wellington's wings and undercarriage, while the fuselage would be a completely new stressed-skin design.

After a year, the prototype VC.1, which was built at Foxwarren and registered as G-AGOK, was ready for its first flight. After being taken by road to nearby Wisley in component form, G-AGOK undertook its maiden flight on 22 June 1945.

The Viking was built in three main production versions: the first was the Mk IA, which retained the Wellingtons fabric-covered geodetic wings and tail; next the Mk I had stressed-skin wings and tail; then the Mk IB, which was 28in longer and could accommodate up to 24 passengers, was also fitted with more powerful Hercules engines. One Viking, G-AJPH, was fitted with Rolls-Royce Nene turbojet engines. A military version for the RAF, designated as the Viking Mk 2, was also built as a VIP transport, several serving the King's Flight.

Service

The Viking entered service with BEA on 20 August 1946 (the airline only having been formed 20 days earlier) on a trial basis on a route from Northolt to Oslo, followed by a more permanent service, also from Northolt, to Copenhagen on 1 September. BEA was destined to be the largest operator of the Viking and would retain the type for eight years in passenger configurations ranging from 27 to 36 seats.

The Viking was a great success, the airliner being sold to numerous independent airlines at home and abroad, plus six different air forces including the Argentine Air Force, the RAAF, the Royal Jordanian Air Force, the Pakistan Air Force and the RAF.

Production

Three Viking prototypes were built with Hercules 130 engines, followed by 50 Viking 1s and 1As and 113 Viking IBs. Military orders included 12 Vikings for the RAF.

Technical data – Viking Mk IA, IB & C Mk 2	
ENGINE	(IA) Two 1,675hp Bristol Hercules 130s; (IB & C Mk 2) Two 1,690hp Hercules 634s
WINGSPAN	89ft 3in
LENGTH	(IA) 62ft 10in; (IB & C Mk 2) 65ft 2in
HEIGHT	19ft 7in (tail down)
WING AREA	882 sq ft
EMPTY WEIGHT	(IA) 22,116lb; (IB) 23,000lb
GROSS WEIGHT	(IA) 33,500lb; (IB & C Mk 2) 34,000lb
MAX SPEED	(IA) 210mph at 10,000ft; (IB) 263mph at 10,000ft
CLIMB RATE	(IA) 1,000ft/min; (1B) 1,500ft/min
SERVICE CEILING	(IA) 22,500ft; (IB) 25,000ft
RANGE	(IA) 1,500 miles at 190mph; (IB & C Mk 2) 1,700 miles at 210mph

Above: The third prototype Vickers Viking, G-AGOM, arrives at Farnborough for the 1948 SBAC show. (*Aeroplane*)

Below left: A great post-war success for Vickers during a period of uncertainty, 163 Vikings were built at Weybridge between 1945 and 1949. (*Aeroplane*)

Below right: The fledgling BEA was the first major operator of the Viking, and Mk IA G-AHOS *Valiant* was one of its early aircraft. This Viking later served with BSAA, BWIA, Independent Air Travel, Eagle, Orion and finally Air Safaris. (*Aeroplane*)

Valetta C Mk 1, C Mk 2, T Mk 3 and T Mk 4

Development

The military variant of the civilian Viking airliner was produced to Air Ministry specification C.9/46. Nicknamed 'the Pig' in RAF circles because of its portly shape, the Valetta gave good service across the globe from 1949 to 1960.

Design

The 158th Viking built was selected to be the prototype Valetta, which was given the military serial VL249. The Valetta differed from its civilian counterpart by having a much stronger fuselage floor, to handle freight, and a pair of big loading doors located on the port side of the aircraft. The undercarriage was strengthened and revised with longer-stroke oleos and a modified fuel system. The Viking's Hercules 634 engines were also replaced by a pair of 1,976hp Hercules 230 powerplants.

The C Mk 1 was a most versatile aircraft, which could be used for carrying troops or freight, supply dropping, glider towing or even casualty evacuation duties. The C Mk 2 was much more refined and was introduced as a passenger transport for carrying nine to 15 passengers in comfort. The aircraft also had a longer range, thanks to an extra 116-gallon fuel tank.

The T Mk 3 was a flying classroom specifically for the training of navigators, but only differed externally by having five extra astrodomes and various aerials along its spine. The final variant, the T Mk 4, was easily distinguishable because of its long nose that contained the radar. Sixteen were converted by Marshall's of Cambridge with upgraded and revised internal fittings.

Service

The Valetta first entered RAF service, as a Dakota replacement, in May 1949 with 204 Squadron at Kabrit. The aircraft later replaced several other Dakota units of Transport Command and those still serving in the Middle and Far East Air Forces. The type first saw action in Malaya with 48, 52 and 110 squadrons, dropping tons of supplies to British troops fighting terrorists in the jungle.

The T Mk 3, which first flew in August 1950, re-equipped five Air Navigation Schools (ANS) and the RAF College Cranwell, while the T Mk 4 only served with 2 ANS and 228 OCU at Leeming.

By 1957, the Valetta was already being replaced by a new generation of heavy transport aircraft, led by the Blackburn Beverly. The Handley Page Hastings also replaced the Valetta which remained in service until August 1960.

Production

In total, 190 Valetta C Mk Is were built, serialled VL263–VL282, VW140–VW206, VW802–VW864, VX483–VX563, WD157–WD171 and WJ491–WJ499; 21 C Mk 2s (VIP) serialled VX571–VX590 and WJ504; 41 T Mk 3s, a prototype was serialled VX564, and the remainder were serialled WG256–WG267 and WJ461–WJ487, (16 T Mk 3s were later converted to T Mk 4 standard); 16 T Mk 4s, serialled WG256, WG263, WG267, WJ464, WJ467, WJ469, WJ471–WJ473, WJ476, WJ477, WJ482, WJ483 and WJ485–WJ487.

Technical data – Valetta C Mk I	
ENGINE	Two 2,000hp Bristol Hercules 230s
WINGSPAN	89ft 3in
LENGTH	62ft 11in
HEIGHT	19ft 7in (tail down)
WING AREA	882 sq ft
EMPTY WEIGHT	24,980lb
GROSS WEIGHT	36,500lb
MAX SPEED	258mph at 10,000ft
CLIMB RATE	1,275ft/min
SERVICE CEILING	21,500ft
RANGE	1,460 miles at 211mph at 10,000ft

Above left: This is Valetta C Mk 1 VL280 serving with 167 Squadron, which was a ferry unit operating out of Abingdon.

Above right: One 'pet pig', Valetta C Mk 1 WJ491, remained on the strength of the A&AEE until the early 1970s, when it was SOC on 10 April 1972. The aircraft was flown to Gatow in West Berlin for fire practice.

Right: This image shows the prototype Valetta T Mk 3, VX564, which served with 1 ANS, 2 ANS, 215 Squadron and the Royal Air Force College (RAFC) before it was SOC in March 1967.

Nene-Viking

Development

There is some conjecture as to which aircraft actually became the world's first jet-powered airliner. Avro would always maintain that its Nene-Lancastrian was the first, but the type's purity is open to question. Not only were the Lancastrian's roots in the Lancaster, but also the fact remains that the aircraft still retained two of its Merlins. This effectively made the aircraft little more than an engine testbed, despite the ability to carry passengers during its many test flights.

Based upon the already-successful Viking Mk IB airframe, the new Type 618 Nene-Viking was designed as a civilian passenger-carrying aircraft from the start. Even while the project was in its infancy, the Ministry of Supply (MoS) showed a great deal of interest in the aircraft, sponsoring the construction and ordering a single aircraft.

Design

The 107th Viking airframe on the Weybridge production line was selected and transported by road to Wisley. All major design changes revolved around the engines and providing a more substantial undercarriage, otherwise the Nene-Viking did not differ a great deal from the standard Mk IB. A pair of 5,000lb Nene I turbojets were mounted below the wing, enabling the jet efflux to pass below the tailplane. Each Nene was housed in a large, aerodynamic pod. The undercarriage was another work of art with a pair of double-wheeled units. Each unit was a twin leg assembly, with a pair of oleo-pneumatic shock absorber legs, supported by knee-joint articulating links. A double-acting hydraulic jack on each side of the aircraft prompted the undercarriage retract, and, as it did, the units split apart with each wheel tucking in either side of the engines jet pipe.

Service

The Nene-Viking was rolled out at Wisley for its first flight on 6 April 1948. Now registered G-AJPH, the aircraft would be flown by Mutt Summers. Taxiing out onto the grass runway, Summers opened the throttles, and after 1,100 yards the aircraft was already 50ft off the ground. Handling was described as satisfactory, although the upper end of the aircraft's performance was yet to be fully discovered.

Up until this time, the Nene-Viking had not been in the public eye despite its significance. However, an opportunity for the aircraft to make a commemorative flight to France, celebrating the 39th Anniversary of Louis Bleriot's flight across the English Channel on 15 July 1909, was grasped. Mutt Summers took off from Heathrow Airport at 10.15am on 15 July 1948. Just 34 minutes 7 seconds later, the Nene-Viking touched down at Villacoublay, an airfield which was used by Bleriot at the time of his record-breaking flight. The 222-mile-long flight was covered at an average speed of 394mph. However, 415mph was briefly attained when the aircraft reached its maximum height for this trip of a mere 12,000ft.

The aircraft went on to spend most of its life with the MoS, including a spell at Boscombe Down as VX856, on 3 March 1949, for Nene engine trials. With very little use for the aircraft and overtaken by technology, it languished at Wisley, until it was sold to Eagle Aviation by the MoS in December 1953. Rebuilt as a Viking Mk IB and returned to the civilian register as G-AJPH, the aircraft entered service with Eagle as *Lord Dundonald* on 24 September 1954. Withdrawn from use on 7 October 1961, the aircraft was placed in store at Heathrow, only to be scrapped the following year. Sadly, this groundbreaking aircraft's remains were dumped in a gravel pit at Bedfont, Feltham, in March 1962.

Technical data – Nene-Viking	
ENGINE	Two 5,000lb Rolls-Royce Nene turbojets
WINGSPAN	89ft 3in
LENGTH	65ft 2in
HEIGHT	19ft 7in
WING AREA	882 sq ft
CRUISING SPEED	395mph
MAX SPEED	468mph
CEILING	40,000ft
MAX RANGE	311 miles at 10,000ft

Right: **Nene-Viking VX856 during Nene engine trials with the A&AEE. Full advantage was taken of the aircraft's outstanding ceiling, and on more than one occasion it was intercepted at high altitude by RAF fighter pilots who were slightly bemused to see a Viking at 40,000ft!**

Below: **The Nene-Viking arriving at the 1948 SBAC at Farnborough. Resplendent in silver, with a bright blue stripe following the line of the passenger windows, matched by a thinner blue stripe along the pods, the Nene- Viking would have been very difficult to overlook. (*Aeroplane*)**

Viscount Prototypes

Development

The Vickers Viscount was arguably the most successful product of the Brabazon Committee; the airliner was a daring, groundbreaking design that fully exploited the very latest form of propulsion – the turboprop. Vickers was convinced this was the way forward, although the Brabazon Committee was not so certain. The specification the aircraft was pitched at was split into two parts: a piston-engined variant, which would be the Airspeed Ambassador, and a turboprop, which would be Rex Pierson's VC.2.

Design

The original specification called for a 24-seat aircraft capable of covering 1,750 miles at 200mph, but when BEA became involved in the project in 1946 it requested that the aircraft have its capacity raised to 32 seats. The original design was basically a four-engined Viking, followed by another proposal for a double-bubble type aircraft like the Vanguard, which would not appear for many years.

On 9 March 1946, Vickers was awarded a contract to Air Ministry specification C.16/46 for two prototypes, which, at first, were to be called the Viceroy – a reference to the Imperial Office of Viceroy in India – but by 1947 that country was independent, and the name Viscount was chosen instead. By 1948, Rex Pierson had died, and the project was now in the hands of George Edwards. He had always favoured the underdeveloped Rolls-Royce Dart for the new airliner, while the Air Ministry wanted the Armstrong Siddeley Mamba, which was a proven powerplant but much heavier than the Dart. To cover both eventualities, the aircraft was designed so that either turboprop could be fitted with little trouble.

Construction of the Type 630 began at Foxwarren in 1946, and within the space of two years the first aircraft, registered as G-AHRF, was ready.

Service

On 16 July 1948, having been transported by road from Foxwarren, the prototype Viscount completed its maiden flight from the grass at Wisley in the safe hands of Mutt Summers. While the aircraft performed as expected, BEA was less than enthusiastic and had already placed an order for 20 Ambassadors. Regardless, flight trials progressed well, and in February 1949, the MoS recognised the potential of the aircraft and ordered a single larger Type 700, which was already under development. G-AHRF went on to gain its CofA in September 1949 and by July 1950 was in service with BEA, providing pilot and ground crew familiarisation, as by then the airline had also recognised the aircraft's potential.

The second prototype, the Type 633, was built as a testbed for a pair of Rolls-Royce Tay turbojets and was registered as G-AMAV at first and then VX217. First flown from Brooklands on 28 August 1950, the aircraft was used for jet engine development for many years.

Production

Two aircraft, the prototype Type 630, G-AHRF, which later flew trials as VX211, and the Type 663 Rolls-Royce Tay turbojet testbed, serialled VZ217, were built. A third 600 series aircraft, registered as G-AJZW and planned with Naiad engines, was not completed, and the components were used for the first 700 series aircraft, G-AMAV.

Technical data – Type 630 Viscount & Type 663 Tay Viscount	
ENGINE	(630) Four 1,380ehp Rolls-Royce Dart R.Da.1 Mk 502s; (663) Two Rolls-Royce Tay turbojets
WINGSPAN	88ft 11in
LENGTH	74ft 6in
HEIGHT	26ft 3in
WING AREA	885 sq ft
EMPTY WEIGHT	29,060lb
GROSS WEIGHT	38,650lb
MAX SPEED	332mph at 10,000ft
MAX RANGE	1,380 miles at 277mph

Above left: The Type 630 Viscount prototype, G-ARHF, in Vickers livery, during an early flight test in the hands of Mutt Summers. (Charles E. Brown via *Aeroplane*)

Above right: With ample power to spare, the Type 630 demonstrates its ability to fly on two of its four turboprops; note the small amount of rudder applied. The aircraft served the Ministry of Supply from 1948 to 1949 as VX211. (Charles E. Brown via *Aeroplane*)

Detail of the prototype's 1,380ehp Rolls-Royce Dart R.Da.1 Mk 502 port outer engine, showing its neat installation and excellent access via the multiple panels.

Varsity T Mk 1

Development

Designed to specification T.13/48 (OR.249), Vickers was well-placed to design a multi-engine trainer to replace the Wellington T Mk 10. While the Varsity was considered more modern than the old 'Wimpy', the aircraft was a natural development of the Viking and Valetta, with one main difference. The Varsity had a tricycle undercarriage, which brought the aircraft up to date with regard to take-off and landing procedures and characteristics, despite many of the machines early customers being destined to fly the big tail draggers still in service, such as the Avro Lincoln, Shackleton and Handley Page Hastings.

Design

The position of the undercarriage brought about the main design changes to the Varsity, which stood it apart from the older short-haul Vickers airliners. To accommodate the nose wheel, the forward fuselage had to be extended and to compensate, the span of the wing was increased by over 6ft. Bomb-aimer training facilities were solved by adding a large pannier below the fuselage, the forward section accommodating the trainee while the rear section could hold up to 24 25lb practice bombs. The Varsity was also equipped with full radar equipment, including H2S and Rebecca.

Service

The prototype, VX828, undertook its maiden flight on 17 July 1949, and in February 1950, the RAF announced it would be placing a large production order. Deliveries began on 1 October 1951, the first customer being 201 AFS at Swinderby, which was operating the Wellington T Mk 10. Serving Flying Training Command, the Varsity not only provided conversion training for pilots, but also advanced training for navigators and bomb-aimers.

The impressive 2,648-mile range of the Varsity allowed the aircraft to carry out long-distance flying training direct to Cyprus, Malta and North Africa, and student aircrews often took part in major air exercises playing the role of enemy bombers.

As well as operating with many training units such as 1 AES, 1 and 2 ANS, 5 and 6 FTS and the RAF College Cranwell, the Varsity also served as part of Signals Command with 97, 115, 116, 151, 173, 187, 192 and 527 squadrons. From 1974, the Scottish Aviation Jetstream was introduced as a more economical crew trainer, but the Varsity still clung on until May 1976.

Production

In total, 163 Varsities were built, including two prototypes, VX828 and VX835 (Type 648), 146 of them at Hurn and 17 at Weybridge. Their serials were in the ranges WF324–WF429, WJ885–WJ950, WL621–WL692 and XD366 (a replacement for WJ900, which was sold to the Swedish Air Force, redesignated as a Tp82 and serialled 82001).

Technical data – Varsity T Mk I	
ENGINE	Two 1,950hp Bristol Hercules 264s
WINGSPAN	95ft 7in
LENGTH	67ft 6in
HEIGHT	23ft 11in
WING AREA	974 sq ft
EMPTY WEIGHT	27,040lb
GROSS WEIGHT	37,500lb
MAX SPEED	288mph at 10,000ft
CLIMB RATE	1,400ft/min
SERVICE CEILING	28,700ft
RANGE	2,648 miles at 239mph

Right: This image shows the first of two prototype Varsities, VX828, built to specification T.13/48, which was initially flown by Mutt Summers and Jock Bryce from Wisley on 17 July 1949.

Below: One of the last bastions of the Varsity was RAF Oakington, which was the home of 5 FTS. These T.1s are on the line during the mid-1970s, not long before the type was withdrawn to make way for the Jetstream. Long serving WF389 'EE' in the foreground was SOC on 12 March 1975.

Type 700 Viscount

Development

The potential of the Type 630 Viscount undoubtedly needed to be expanded upon, and BEA was interested in operating a higher capacity version, with accommodation for up to 43 passengers. The only way this could be achieved was by fitting uprated Dart engines; thankfully, Rolls-Royce offered a new engine, the R.Da.3, at the same time as the competing Airspeed Ambassador was delayed by structural problems.

Design

The slightly bigger proportions of the new aircraft would raise the gross weight of the airliner by 6,500lbs, and, when carrying the maximum 43 passengers, a cruising speed of 333mph could be achieved. Working closely with BEA, a new specification was drawn up for the proposed airliner, which would be designated as the Type 700 Viscount. On 24 February 1949, a single prototype was ordered by the MoS, followed by specification 21/49, which was issued on 19 April 1949.

Construction of the Type 700 was fairly rapid, as major components, which were intended for the third Type 609 prototype, were diverted to this aircraft instead. As a result, it was ready within 18 months, and on 28 August 1950, the prototype, registered G-AMAV, was first flown out of Brooklands by Jock Bryce, on a short journey to neighbouring Wisley for flight testing. The size difference compared to the earlier 600 series Viscounts was obvious; the wingspan was greater by 5ft, and the fuselage was 7ft 4in longer.

Service

BEA placed an order for 20 Type 701 Viscounts on 3 August 1950, which was a slightly upgraded version of the Type 700, able to accommodate 47 passengers in five-abreast seating. On 20 August 1952, the first production aircraft, Type 701 G-ALWE, completed its maiden flight, and then on 3 January 1953, it was delivered to BEA as the first aircraft of the airline's new Discovery Class. The type's CofA was issued on 17 April 1953, and the following day Viscount, G-AMNY named *RMA Sir Ernest Shackleton*, began the world's first regular turboprop service by flying the London, Rome, Athens and Nicosia route.

Following the initial BEA order, which was increased to 26 aircraft, there was a 15-month lull until November 1951 when orders suddenly began to roll in, beginning with 12 Type 708s for Air France and four Type 707s for Aer Lingus. Six months later, Trans-Australian Airlines ordered six Type 720s, but one of the big breakthroughs into the world market came in November 1952, when Trans-Canada Air Lines placed an order for 15 Type 724s. A host of independent operators would also order the Type 700, the first of them in May 1953 when Hunting Clan ordered three Type 732s.

Eventually, 287 Type 700 series were built, making it the most abundant Viscount model by far; the aircraft serving with a host of airlines and several air forces across the world until the late 1990s.

Technical data – V.700 (720) Viscount	
ENGINE	Four 1,740ehp Dart R.Da.3 Mk 506s
WINGSPAN	93ft 8½in
LENGTH	81ft 10in
HEIGHT	26ft 9in
WING AREA	963 sq ft
EMPTY WEIGHT	38,358lb
GROSS WEIGHT	64,500lb
MAX SPEED	380mph (Cruise) at 10,000ft
MAX RANGE	2,000 miles at 317mph

Right: This is Type 700 series BEA production in full swing at Hurn, which lasted from 1950 through to 16 April 1959, when Type 757 CF-TIG was flown out of the Dorset airfield for Trans-Canada Air Lines. (*Aeroplane*)

Below: The Vickers Type 745D Viscount demonstrator, G-APLX, pictured outside one of the erecting shops at Hurn. The aircraft was originally sold to Capital Airlines as N7468 in the USA, but this was not completed, and the aircraft was re-registered as G-APLX on 17 April 1958. (*Aeroplane*)

Valiant, B Mk 1, B(PR) Mk 1, B(PR)K Mk 1 and B Mk 2

Development

In late 1944, the first of many committees met to discuss the future of bomber aircraft and their tactics. Thinking at that time tended to revolve around the current Bomber Command strategy of using massed formations of heavy four-engined aircraft. However, in 1946, things moved forward when Operational Requirements OR229 and OR230 were issued for the development of a new turbojet powered nuclear bomber; the first of these would be the Vickers Valiant.

Design

The Valiant was designed to Air Ministry specification B.9/48, and Vickers was quick off the mark as the prototype, WB210, undertook its maiden flight on 18 May 1951. This aircraft was lost during a test flight over Hampshire on 12 January 1952, but a second prototype, WB215, was already at an advanced stage, completing its maiden flight on 11 April 1952.

The first aircraft was powered by four 6,500lb Avon RA3 turbojets, which had very narrow slot-type intakes. These were expanded on the second prototype and, progressively, more powerful engines were installed into the second aircraft up to the 9,500lb RA14, which would be fitted to early production aircraft.

The production aircraft differed by having longer jet pipes, a dielectric panelled nose and large auxiliary fuel tanks under each wing for long-range operations. The first preproduction B Mk 1, WP199, made its first flight on 22 December 1953.

One B Mk 2 was built, WJ954, which first flew on 4 September 1953, and because of its all-black finish the aircraft was nicknamed the 'Black Bomber'. Superior in performance to the B Mk 1, especially at low-level, the aircraft was designed for a Pathfinder role. However, the concept, according to the Air Ministry, had no place in the nuclear age.

Service

The Valiant B Mk 1 entered service with 138 Squadron at RAF Gaydon in February 1955, the aircraft making its first public appearance in strength at that year's SBAC at Farnborough. Three versions of the Valiant would enter RAF service, the B Mk 1 being followed by the photo-reconnaissance B(PR) Mk 1, which first joined 543 Squadron in July 1955. A tanker variant followed, complete with probe-and-drogue air-to-air refuelling capability, being designated as the B(PR)K Mk 1. The first example flew on 8 May 1956 and entered service with 214 Squadron in February 1958.

Valiants of 138, 148, 207 and 214 squadrons were the first 'V-Bombers' to see action when they took part in the Suez Crisis in October and November 1956; operating from RAF Luqa, Malta, the aircraft dropped standard 1,000lb HE bombs. The Valiant scored another first when WZ366, of 49 Squadron, dropped Britain's first operational atomic bomb on 11 October 1956. Later, Britain's first thermonuclear H-bomb was tested by XD818 on 15 May 1957.

A change of role from high-level to low-level saw the anti-flash, all-white Valiants painted in toned-down camouflage. This role change contributed to the premature demise of the aircraft by putting severe strain on the airframe, which accelerated metal fatigue and resulted in the whole fleet being grounded in late 1964. By February 1965, the type had been withdrawn and within months the majority were scrapped.

Production

A total of 104 Valiants were built, including three prototypes: WB210 (Type 660); WB215 (Type 667); and B Mk 2, WJ954 (Type 673). Production aircraft were serialled WP199–WP223 (pre-production), WZ361–WZ405 and XD812–XD875.

Technical data – Valiant	
ENGINE	(Proto) Four 6,500lb Rolls-Royce Avon RA3s; (B(PR) Mk 1 & B Mk 2) Four 9,500lb Avon RA14 9,500lbs; (B (K) Mk 1) Four 10,500lb Avon 205s
WINGSPAN	114ft 4in
LENGTH	108ft 3in
HEIGHT	32ft 2in
WING AREA	2,362 sq ft
EMPTY WEIGHT	75,881lb
GROSS WEIGHT	140,000lb
MAX SPEED	(B Mk 1) 567mph at 30,000ft; (B Mk 2) 580mph at low level
INITIAL CLIMB	4,000ft/min
SERVICE CEILING	54,000ft
RANGE	(with underwing tanks) 4,500 miles

Above left: Vickers Valiant B(K) Mk I, XD823, was one of a batch of 38 of the mark built at Weybridge. They were all delivered to the RAF between July 1956 and September 1957; XD823 going to 49 Squadron where it remained until SOC on 1 March 1965.

Above right: The prototype Valiant, WB210, undertook its maiden flight on 18 May 1951, only to be lost on 12 January 1952, following an in-flight fire over Hampshire. Four of the five crew managed to escape the aircraft before it plunged into Harrow Wood, five miles northeast of Christchurch.

Right: Valiant B(PR)K Mk 1s of 543 Squadron enjoy one of many overseas detachments from their home station at RAF Wyton. (*Aeroplane*)

Type 800 Viscount

Development

Once again, the future development of the Viscount lay with the engines, which by early 1953 were proceeding at a good pace. Rolls-Royce could now offer the 1,690hp Dart R.Da.5 providing the option of an even larger Viscount, capable of carrying 86 'tourist class' passengers, which would be designated as the Type 800 series.

Design

BEA placed an order for the Type 801 in February 1953, which was planned to be powered by the R.Da.5 and would be 13ft 3in longer than a standard Type 701. While the Type 801 was never built, the design led to the successful Type 802, which served BEA, and the later Type 810. Both variants raised the Viscount's all-up weight and utilised even higher-powered turboprops.

By April 1954, another Dart engine was available and BEA's original order for the Type 801 was replaced by a firm order for a dozen 1,740hp Dart 510-powered Type 802s. The aircraft ended up being just 3ft 10in longer than the Type 701, with the Viscount design adjusted by internally repositioning the rear pressure bulkhead aft by 9ft 3in. The aircraft was now capable of carrying 57 passengers in standard density seating and 65 in a high-density configuration. The 800 series also introduced new rectangular access doors that could double as passenger or freight doors.

A proposed Type 840 Viscount capable of 400mph and powered by the 2,395hp Dart 541 never came to fruition, but it did lead to the Viscount Major 850 project (later Type 870), which in turn produced the next generation of Vickers turboprops – the Vickers Vanguard.

Service

BEA was once again the largest operator of the Type 800 series of Viscounts, of which 67 were built, followed by another 84 with 1,990hp Dart 525 engines, designated as the Type 810. Many major operators used the Type 810, such as All Nippon Airways, Ansett-ANA (Australia), Austrian Airlines, Cubana, Ghana Airways, KLM, Lufthansa, Pakistan International Airlines, South African Airways, Trans-Australia Airlines and VASP, not to mention numerous independent operators.

Production of the Type 800 series did not come to an end until 1964, when the last of 445 aircraft sold; a Type 843 for CAAC (Civil Aviation Administration of China), flew out of Hurn on 2 January. Thus ended one of Britain's most successful aviation stories, raising £177 million in sales and seeing more than 60 different operators, from 40 different countries, purchase the Viscount from new. However, it would be another 30 years before the sound of a quartet of Dart turboprops, running in harmony, left our skies.

Technical data – V.800 (810) Viscount	
ENGINE	Four 1,990ehp Dart R.Da.7/1 Mk 525s
WINGSPAN	93ft 8½in
LENGTH	85ft 8in
HEIGHT	26ft 9in
WING AREA	963 sq ft
EMPTY WEIGHT	43,500lb
GROSS WEIGHT	72,500lb
MAX SPEED	357mph all at 10,000ft
MAX RANGE	1,610 miles at 333mph

Above left: The very first Type 800 series aircraft was not really a prototype but was more the first production aircraft. Designated as the Type 802, G-AOJA was built at Hurn but was transported by road to Weybridge, where it was reassembled to undertake its maiden flight, lasting 35 minutes, to Wisley on 27 July 1956. (*Aeroplane*)

Above right: KLM Royal Dutch Airlines operated nine Type 800 Viscounts between June 1957 and February 1967, including PH-VID. Named after famous early aviator Otto Lilienthal, PH-VID was sold to Aer Lingus on 1 February 1967. (*Aeroplane*)

This is the interior of a BEA Type 802 Viscount, showing the five-abreast seating arrangement, which could be laid out in either 57- or 65-seat configurations. A little cautious at first, BEA went on to be one of the biggest Viscount operators, the airliner serving from July 1950 until April 1974.

Vanguard and Merchantman (Cargoliner)

Development

Not long after the Viscount entered service with BEA, discussions were held with the airline in April 1953 for a potential successor, which could be ready by 1959. A developed version of the Type 701 Viscount was considered at one stage, however, it was clear that a completely new, and much larger aircraft would be needed.

Design

The core of the design evolved from the Type 870 Viscount, which was planned for the new, powerful Rolls-Royce RB109 engine, later to be better known as the Tyne. Once the basic configuration of the aircraft was decided, including a double-bubble fuselage, the new airliner was designated as the Type 950. Named the Vanguard, the new airliner could fly almost twice as high as the Viscount and was considerably faster; in fact, it was one of the world's fastest turboprops. Orders for the aircraft were first received from BEA in July 1956.

The Type 950 was designed with a gross weight of 135,000lb and as production Type 951, the aircraft was configured to carry 127 passengers. Trans-Canada Airlines (TCA) also showed an interest in the Vanguard, but its requirements were for an aircraft with a greater payload, with the carriage of freight being the priority rather than passengers. This aircraft was the Type 952, which was fitted with more powerful engines and a stronger fuselage, allowing it to carry a payload of 24,000lb or 139 passengers.

The Type 953 followed for BEA, which was fitted with the same engines as the Type 951 but used the sturdier airframe of the Type 952. The aircraft could carry a payload of 29,000lb or up to 135 passengers. The final variant, which came about when Air Canada converted several of its aircraft to an all-freight configuration, was the Type 953C Merchantman. In Canadian service, the aircraft was known as the Cargoliner.

Service

BEA and TCA received their first Vanguards from 1960, the former beginning scheduled services on 17 December from Heathrow to Paris. Once all had been delivered to BEA by March 1962, the type took over the majority of UK and European routes. Passenger flights continued briefly after the British Airways takeover of BEA in April 1974, but it was the Merchantman that continued to serve until 1979. The Canadian Cargoliners had a shorter life, the majority had been withdrawn in 1972, but in the UK the remaining few Merchantman continued to serve with Air Bridge Carriers until 1996.

Production

In total, 44 were built, including one Type 950 prototype and a pair of static test fuselages; six Type 951s were built for BEA, 23 Type 952s for TCA; and 14 Type 953s for BEA. Nine Type 953s were converted into Merchantman aircraft and were redesignated as the Type 953C.

Technical data – Vanguard 951, 952 & 953	
ENGINE	(951 & 953) Four 4,985ehp Rolls-Royce Tyne RTy1 Mk 506s; (952) Four 5,545ehp Tyne RTy11 Mk 512s
WINGSPAN	118ft
LENGTH	122ft 10½in
HEIGHT	34ft 11in
WING AREA	1,527 sq ft
EMPTY WEIGHT	(951) 84,000lb; (952 & 953) 85,000lb
GROSS WEIGHT	(951) 135,000lb; (952 & 953) 141,000lb
MAX SPEED	(951 & 952) 400mph; (953) 425mph
MAX RANGE	(951) 1,550 miles at 380mph at 21,000ft; (952) 1,830 miles at 412mph at 20,000ft; (953) 2,070 miles at 412mph at 20,000ft

Above left: The second BEA Vanguard was G-APEB, seen here en route to the SBAC show at Farnborough in September 1959, where the aircraft made its British public debut. (*Aeroplane*)

Above right: The prototype Vanguard, G-AOYW, after being rolled out at Weybridge on 4 December 1958.

Below left: A brand new Merchantman belonging to BEA Cargo, pictured in 1969, presents us with a good view of the large forward cargo door.

Below right: Hunting Air Cargo's Merchantman, G-APEP *Superb*, makes a low pass over the remainder of Brooklands' short runway before landing on 17 October 1996. The last of the breed to fly, the aircraft remained in taxiable condition until May 2004, when it was moved over 'the bridge', where it remains today in the Brooklands Museum Vickers Aircraft Park. (*Aeroplane*)

VC10, C Mk 1, C Mk 1K, K Mk 2 to 4

Development

Only surpassed in speed by Concorde, the VC10 remains the fastest airliner in the world. Its roots lay in the ill-fated V1000 project, which was due to fly in 1955, but, like so many Government-backed projects, it had the plug pulled at an advanced stage of construction. Features designed into the V1000, such as a variable-incidence tailplane, power-operated flying control surfaces and even its integrally machined wing members would all be incorporated into the VC10. Furthermore, knowledge and experience gained from the Viscount and later Vanguard would see the VC10 embody every ounce of technology Vickers had accumulated during the post-war period.

Design

In March 1957, a specification was issued by BOAC for an airliner capable of operating on routes to Africa and Australia, which could carry approximately 35,000lb over 4,000 miles. From this point forward, the VC10 would be built to BOAC's parameters alone, which would sadly, in hindsight, limit the appeal of the aircraft to other operators. A great deal of focus was placed on the aircraft's short field ability, but subtle changes in the design, such as increasing the sweep of the wings by the smallest margin, gave the aircraft the ability to carry out transatlantic services with ease.

The prototype, designated as the Type 1100, was fitted with a quartet of 21,000lb Conway engines and was first flown out of the tight confines of Brooklands by Jock Bryce, Brian Trubshaw and flight engineer Bill Cairns on 29 June 1962. After entering service with BOAC, a new Super VC10 was designed, which was 13ft longer than the original aircraft, raising the capacity from 135 to 163 passengers. Further developmental changes included the provision of a large side-loading freight door, making the aircraft particularly appealing to the RAF, which had expected to receive the V1000. The RAF went on to order 14 C Mk 1s (Type 1106s), all but one later being converted to have a dual tanker/transport capability. Many more, all ex-civilian, aircraft were converted to K Mk 1, 2 and 3 standard, the latter two marks being able to refuel from three refuelling points.

Service

The VC10 was introduced to regular passenger services from London–Lagos by BOAC from 29 April 1964. It quickly took over all of the African, Middle Eastern and Far Eastern routes, while the Super VC10 plied the North Atlantic from London–New York. Three VC10s were later built for Ghana Airways and a pair for British United, while an order for Nigeria Airways fell through. The prototype was converted to a Type 1109 for Laker Airways.

The RAF received its first aircraft in July 1966 and, after 47 years' service, the it retired its final four aircraft in September 2013.

Production

In total, 54 aircraft were built, beginning with a single Type 1100 prototype; 12 Type 1101s; three Type 1102s; two Type 1103s; one Type 1109 (Type 1100 converted); 17 Type 1151s (Super VC10); and five Type 1154s. The RAF ordered 14 Type 1106 C Mk 1s (13 later converted to C Mk 1K [Type 1180]); five Type 1112 K Mk 2s (ex-Type 1101); four Type 1164 K Mk 3s (ex-Type 1154) and five Type 1170 K Mk 4s (ex-Type 1151).

Technical data – VC10 (1101), Super VC10 (1151) & C Mk I (1106)	
ENGINE	(1101) Four 21,000lb Rolls-Royce Conway RCo42s; (1151 & 1106) Four 22,500lb Conway RCo43s
WINGSPAN	146ft 2in
LENGTH	158ft 8in
HEIGHT	39ft 6in
WING AREA	2,932 sq ft
EMPTY WEIGHT	(1101) 139,505lb; (1151) 146,962lb; (1106) 142,220lb
GROSS WEIGHT	(1101) 312,000lb; (1151) 335,000lb; (1106) 322,000lb
MAX CRUISING SPEED	580mph
SERVICE CEILING	38,000ft
MAX RANGE	(1101) 5,850 miles; (1151) 5,960 miles; (1106) 6,260 miles

One of the most beautiful airliners ever built, VC10 G-ARTA is banked away from the camera ship by Jock Bryce during an early test flight in 1962. Although the aircraft was displayed in BOAC markings, the aircraft never joined the airline but was sold to Freddie Laker as a Type 1109. Laker leased the aircraft to Middle East Airways before it joined British Caledonian. (*Aeroplane*)

The first of just 54 VC10s built was Type 1101 G-ARTA, pictured outside of the Weybridge factory prior to its dramatic first flight on 29 June 1962. (*Aeroplane*)

The Vickers-Armstrongs V.1000 (VC7)

Worthy of mention is another aircraft that could not only have transformed the face of British aviation, but also the path of commercial air travel across the world. The story, which only lasted for a period of four years, began in 1951 when the MoS asked Vickers if it would consider designing an RAF transport derivative of the Valiant bomber.

The result was the Vickers Type 1000, aka the VC7, which made use of the wings of the Valiant complete with a wide, six-abreast fuselage, of similar design to the Comet, but on a grander scale. There was nothing like the VC7 in the world at the time, and the design really rattled the American manufacturers, Boeing and Douglas, whose future 707 and DC-8 airliners had much less capacity. The VC7 forced both manufacturers to rethink their original designs, because carriers at the time were only interested in the Vickers' aircraft.

Construction of the prototype began in February 1953, with plans for the maiden flight to take place in December 1955. BOAC was very interested in the VC7, despite having already ordered the Britannia, several of which, significantly, were to be built by Short Brothers in Belfast. By late 1955, the VC7 was by far the most expensive project being undertaken and under government orders, the Air Staff were instructed to make some radical cuts to save money. Short Brothers were desperate for work following the cancellation of the Swift and the Comet 2, while the Britannia, which was also ordered by the RAF, would save the company from laying off hundreds of Northern Irish workers. So once again, events, which still occur today, befell the promising VC7; marking the beginning of the end of British aircraft manufacturing industry in many people's eyes.

Technical data – V.1000 (Civil 100 Passenger Version)	
ENGINE	(Proposals) Four 15,550lb Rolls-Royce Conway RCo3s; Four 14,500lb Conway RCo5s with reheat; Six 12,800lb RCo5s; Four 19,650lb RB125s or Four 17,300lb Bristol BOL7s
WINGSPAN	140ft
LENGTH	146ft
HEIGHT	(to fin tip) 38ft 6in
WING AREA	3,263 sq ft
WEIGHT	(less fuel and payload) 109,100lb
MAX TAKE-OFF WEIGHT	231,000lb
MAX LANDING WEIGHT	149,00lb
CRUISING SPEED	450 kts
MEAN CEILING	(Medium-range domestic) 40,000ft
MAX RANGE	(Medium-range domestic) 2,000 miles with max payload of 24,900lb

In early 1955, the RAF was so keen to get its hands on the VC7 that a production order, under contract 6/Air/11190/C.B.6(c), was placed for six aircraft, to be serialled XH255–XH260. (*Aeroplane*)

Yet another great British design was erased from history in November 1955, when the VC7 was cancelled because of a cost-cutting exercise. The near-complete prototype remained at Wisley until 1957, when it was cut into 20–25ft long sections and transported to Shoeburyness so that the Proof & Experimental Establishment could carry out vulnerability trials. (*Aeroplane*)

Other books you might like:

Aviation Industry Series,
Vol. 1

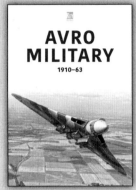

Aviation Industry Series,
Vol. 3

Aviation Industry Series,
Vol. 2

For our full range of titles please visit:
shop.keypublishing.com/books